# The Water Holds No Scars

# The Water Holds No Scars

## Fly Fishing Stories of Rivers & Rejuvenation

edited by

Dean K Miller

TULIPTREE
PUBLISHING, LLC

ISBN-13: 978-0692583586

ISBN-10: 0692583580

TulipTree Publishing, LLC

Sterling, Colorado

Designed and typeset by
TulipTree Publishing, LLC / tuliptreepub.com

Unless otherwise noted, all photos are by Dean K Miller / deankmiller.com
Photos on pp. 132 & 136 by Louis Phillippe

The publisher makes no representations as to the truth or fiction of each piece.
These are fishing stories, after all.

To my father, Cecil W. Miller,

who took me fishing.

# Contents

# Contents

# In thanks...

To all the fish, the beautiful places they reside,
and the moments of joy, recovery, peace, and smiles
our interactions with them have provided.

# Editor's Welcome

## Dean K Miller

After five and a half decades of life, and most of them spent fishing, I've come to wonder what keeps bringing those of us who fish, back to the water time and time again. Sure, some of the answers are easy: nature, friends, trophy fish, and simple things like that. But certainly there must be more.

When I ask my fly fishing friends why they enjoy the sport so much, their first reaction is usually one of silence as I see them drift into their thoughts. Usually there's a measure of uncertainty in their answers. Maybe they haven't thought about it much, or the "it," whatever "it" is, is ingrained deep in our psyche and souls and they are hesitant to share something so intimate with another.

In my work with military veterans through Project Healing Waters Fly Fishing,

I've seen incredible transitions in short periods of time on the water. Catching a fish isn't necessary to find this special connection between human and water, between heart and self. After a fly fishing trip, many veterans, when asked, will state the events of the day, the changes they experience, and the benefits they receive. But often they, too, are unable to uniquely express the compelling reasons why fly fishing affects them so deeply.

I've heard that a well-timed fly cast matches the rhythm of an at-rest heartbeat. Maybe that's what opens the door. This collection of essays and stories from both veterans and non-veterans explores what happens when we walk through that open door. Their tales are as diverse as the writers themselves. The heartfelt stories of their struggles, joys, and solace arrive at a level of honesty that only those bearing witness can describe.

Maybe we can't fully answer the question "Why do we fish?" But I'm willing to continue exploring the rivers, lakes, and streams of rejuvenation in my quest to better know myself. You're welcome to join me anytime.

# Hope

## Matthew Starr

In the deep darkness

those moments before dawn,

we lay restless

waiting for dreams to end

so we may wake

and set forth

to hope,

to live.

We wake with the sun
narrow rods of light
streaming straight through windows,
reflecting ambition
swimming warm in our soul
and we smile
knowing with the knowledge of promise
the day will be good.
Patiently we gather
the tools of our craft
providing reality
to the late dreams
so recently vanished
in our minds.
When we find our way
to where the river runs through
we step into flowing
waters of conviction.
Silver and slippery,
our quarry awaits
that devilish meal
so clever and deceiving
we've prepared.

The winds are still.

The distant trees quiet.

A bird sings

for love and life.

The heart casts out.

Casting, casting, casting,

the heart yearns

for the tugging of the line

between hope and reality.

But the line is slack.

Light is failing.

With the setting of the sun

hope fades.

Night falls

and we must return another day

to begin again

once more.

We live.

# Moving Water

## S. R. Kinsella

When I stand alone, toe deep at the edge of a trout stream on a summer day, the water lapping against the laces of my wading boots, something magical and mysterious happens. The rhythmic slosh of water coupled with the heat fills me with a sense of comfort and peace. Sound and warmth, warmth and sound, a soft, gentle swirl. It's not so much a transformation as it is a journey—a journey to a place that is familiar yet, unlike the water about my feet, never fully in reach.

I have always loved moving water. One of my earliest memories of it was at the age of four or five standing thigh deep in the swirling brown pulse of the Missouri River a mile from my home. I, and a couple of older friends (I think they were six), walked to the river, unbeknownst to our parents. There we stood, almost one with the river, the current

pushing hard against our legs, as fragments of driftwood and a trail of foam raced by. We never knew we were in danger; we felt worldly and in complete control of ourselves, the sharp, earthy smell of the river and the towering cottonwoods it nourished hanging in the air around us. We lingered far longer than we had intended, finally leaving reluctantly to race back before someone we knew discovered us. Years later, when I recounted that day's adventure to my mother, she gasped.

As I grew older, even though we moved away from the Missouri River, a stream or a river was never far away. In grade school and junior high, my friends and I would sometimes bike or walk miles to get to the small creeks and rivers that wound through prairie and corn fields on the edge of my hometown on the Great Plains. There, we would fish for carp, bullheads, catfish, and the occasional crappie or bass. Sometimes we went to a favorite small creek just to watch the herons and mink that would wade and scurry about the creek, providing a beautiful yet tragic contrast to the nearby sound of bulldozers and backhoes carving up a housing development on the hills above it. Sometimes we just went there to smoke cigarettes pilfered from a parent's dresser drawer, taking in the sounds and the movement of the water as we talked about what we would do and where we would go the minute we graduated from high school and could escape the flat, dry town we lived in. Most of my friends opted for construction jobs in Alaska and Wyoming with their mountain-broken landscapes; I chose college.

When I was eighteen, I moved to a small university town that stands on the bluffs above one of the last remaining wild sections of the Missouri River. It was down river from a wall of earth, concrete, and rock that had been erected in the late 1940s and early '50s by the U.S. Army Corps of Engineers—the federal agency that had come to champion what it viewed as a worthy and important mission to place high-dollar chokeholds around some of the nation's wildest and most beautiful rivers—and upstream from the unnatural channels that had been carved into the river to accommodate commercial barges. Being that close once again to the Missouri River became an excuse to skip class on warm days—although I seldom needed an excuse. We would swim out to the wild sandbars that shifted day by day like water-saturated dunes. There we played touch football; or lay in the warm, muddy sand, drank cheap beer, and watched the clouds drift by; or used a piece of driftwood to show the world (or at least low-flying airplanes) our broadening university-based knowledge by writing in five-foot letters, along the long expanse of a sandbar, philosophical musings about life and learning.

Grizzly bears once wandered the banks of the Missouri River where we swam, as did elk. William Clark recorded in his journal that he saw many signs of elk in the area as he and Meriwether Lewis and their fellow explorers moved up the river. The grizzlies and the elk are long gone, but their ancient aquatic brethren—the paddlefish, gar, and sturgeon—still remain, protected by a thin watery barrier from the two-leggeds who plowed fields, paved roads, straightened the river, and built massive earthen dams.

Rivers and moving water continued to wander in and out of my life for years after I left college. And then I discovered fly fishing for trout. I had long fished more for an opportunity to be near moving water than as a serious vocation. One summer day, I watched an angler standing waist deep in a small river, line in the air, casting an undiscernible fly to rising fish, some of which visibly broke the surface in pursuit of the fly. He was not only fishing the water, he was part of it! Within weeks I gave up my spin-casting rods and bought a cheap fly rod and a set of waders and flies.

It was on the third or fourth time I went fly fishing, when I slowed down and quit focusing so much on technique, that I discovered something even greater. Healthy trout streams explode with life, and that life, combined with the water, emits an aroma that is part water, part earth, and part life. As a fly angler you imitate small fragments of that life—nymph, mayfly, minnow, mouse—and become one with the river and its fish. But it's the smell of a trout stream that makes it distinguishable from any other piece of moving water. It comes back to you every time you return to a river or stream and step back into the water. It's like the familiar, intoxicating aroma of the neck of a former lover you hooked up with again. The water, its movement, its smell. I feel unhealthy and unbalanced if too much time has passed since I have stood toe deep in a trout river.

I am not alone in my love for rivers. Poets and writers and philosophers have long immortalized the tie humans have with moving water. Do a Google search of "poems about rivers" or "writings about rivers" or "river stories" and the results seem almost without end. Dickinson, Thoreau, Longfellow, Kipling, Angelou, Hemingway. Indeed, one of the earliest known human writings—the Sumerian Script—was created in the fertile river valley of the Euphrates and Tigris Rivers. The script for water was an outgrowth of the image of flowing water—a river. Maybe the Sumerians created a written language, in part, because they too were inspired by moving water?

Humans are one with water, especially moving water. We always have been. It is with us from before birth. A child in utero develops its ears at about eight weeks. A few weeks after that, it begins to hear its first two sounds—the rythmic beat of its mother's heart and the flow of blood being whooshed river-like through the umbilical cord.

When my son was just a few weeks old he suffered from colic—the mysterious, parent-frustrating affliction that causes an otherwise healthy infant to fuss and cry. My wife and I would rock him, feed him, and rub his back, but little seemed to work. When human interaction failed, I opted for technology, investing in a small plastic audio device that emitted a dozen different sounds. I brought it home, plugged it in next to his crib, and pushed the "white noise" button. He squirmed and fussed. I pushed the button for the sound of a heartbeat, which startled him. I tried several other sounds, with little positive reaction. About to give up, thinking that the purchase was ridiculous, I pushed the button marked "mountain stream." The device emitted a gurgling, rushing sound. He stopped moving, turned in the direction of the sound, and looked in the air searching, not so much for its source it seemed, but for his connection to its familiarity. He calmed and fell asleep. For months the machine sat by his crib for use whenever he began to fuss and cry. I still have it in my closet.

Even in the afterlife, humans and rivers are sometimes inseparable. In Western cultures, the dead are buried, a tradition that carries forward in spite of the increasing popularity of cremation. But in other cultures, rivers and death are just as intertwined as rivers and life are. The Hindus and some Buddhists immerse the cremated remains of their dead in rivers as an offering to the gods, to be carried away to become part of the river. I have read that for some Hindus, the chosen place of death is along the bank of a river, preferably one they hold sacred, to have the aura of a river in their last breath.

I am not a Hindu; I am a fallen Catholic. But if I could choose a place to die it would be on the bank of one of the trout streams I have long held sacred in the Black Hills of South Dakota. The unmistakable odor of trout water in my nostrils, the sound of its rolling, gurgling flow in my ears, the heat of the sun warming my body. And then I die, my soggy, decomposing body feeding the worms and insects that will feed the trout, giving something back to the earth as my final act rather than just taking something away, as we humans have become so adept at doing.

Long before our ancestors Homo erectus and the Java and Peking people with their stone tools, long before their ancestors, the upright primates who had the unique ability to both walk on the ground and climb trees to evade enemies, water was our home. Roughly four hundred million years ago our ancestors began to crawl out from their watery stations to venture in search of the opportunities that the great shifting land masses provided. The ancestors of all mammals—including us—had legs and lungs *and* gills. They could breathe in the water, and, for short periods of time, out of the water. It was as though they couldn't decide to be animals of the water or animals of the land, and the evolutionary process was helping them hedge their bets. Eventually the lungs won out and the gills disappeared. Can it be that some thread of ancient genetic material makes us one with the land *and* water? Maybe the comfort we get from a flowing river is because of a fragment of genetic memory of the safety and comfort we had surrounded by warm flowing, embryotic-like water before our gills disappeared.

I am not alone in my love of moving water. Amidst its updates and fundraising appeals, the conservation organization American Rivers has on its website a page of river quotes—which they oddly entitled "Famous Quotes about Rivers." Among the quotes from politicians and newscasters and others (maybe it should have been entitled "river quotes from famous people" but I guess that doesn't read as poetically) is this statement from John Muir, one of America's first naturalists and himself an admirer of rivers: "Rivers flow not past, but through us."

Rivers do indeed flow through us. Maybe that's why I prefer to fish without human companions. Because when I stand alone, toe deep in a river, it flows through me, and with it my past, my present, my future, and everything around me. When I stand next to moving water I am one with all humanity, one with all living things. I breathe the earthy water in through my lungs, holding it, finally releasing it, retaining its magical essence. Sound and warmth, warmth and sound, a soft, gentle swirl. When I stand next to a river, I am never alone.

*Steve Kinsella is a writer, communications consultant, and avid fly angler living in Saint Paul, Minnesota. He served as the former editor of* TROUT, *Trout Unlimited's award-winning quarterly magazine, and his book,* 900 Miles from Nowhere: Voices from the Homestead Frontier *(Minnesota Historical Society Press), was a finalist for the Great Plains Book Award. He is also the author of* Trout Fishing the Black Hills. *His clients have included Trout Unlimited's Western Water Project, Montana Trout Unlimited, and the Theodore Roosevelt Conservation Partnership.*

# Mitchell Creek Legacy

## Duane Cook

As early as 1892, Mitchell, Colorado, was an important siding on the Tennessee Pass line of the Denver & Rio Grande railroad. It sits near the top of the steep 3 percent grade that leads to Tennessee Pass and the welcome descent toward Pueblo. The narrow canyons and ledges of the line make a smooth transition as the tracks reach the valley below Slide Mountain. This location provided enough room to support a double track operation with depot, shops, coke ovens, living quarters, and a thriving population. All of this was possible because of Mitchell Creek and the water needed to run a railroad operation in those early days. It is this same stream that is the fishing legacy of my family.

I grew up at Tennessee Pass, eight miles from the nearest town in the middle of the Colorado Rockies, where the climate could best be summed up as seven months of winter, two months of bad snow, and three of the most splendid months of fishing and summer that one can imagine! It was here, as a four-year-old, one day from going to the hospital to have my tonsils taken out, that my father stopped the family car and took me to the "bottom hole" on Mitchell Creek to try my luck at catching my first fish. Later I would learn this was one of my dad's favorite spots on the creek because it was so close to the highway that few fishermen thought there were fish in the water. They were sure wrong. I made only three casts, with some help, before I had a rainbow in the creel and headed back to the warmth of the backseat of the family Chevrolet and the short ride home. That memory of my first fish, with my dad, in that spot, is burned indelible in my mind.

Throughout our time at Tennessee Pass I fished that two-mile stretch of Mitchell Creek too many times to count. Each time, the bottom hole was not just the finish of the journey, but the spot to catch that proverbial last fish. I cannot say that there was always a hook-up finish to end the day, but more often than not, I was able to relive that first fish experience.

Fast-forward some ten years to my return from Vietnam. It was a time that changed me forever, as war does to most who live that nightmare. To make matters worse, I returned in December and the weather was miserable. Staying inside is not a good thing for those returning from conflict, as it leads to way too much down time in which the mind begins to venture in directions that have no good end. The one flash that kept me going through that first winter was the thought of spring and the bottom hole.

I knew that it would be at least mid-May before all the snow was gone from Tennessee Pass. I could not wait. My birthday is the end of April and I decided that would be the time to resume the legacy. I hiked through thigh-deep snow to get to the spot, not even knowing if it was open, but it was, and after an hour I set the hook on a nice twelve-inch rainbow. This time I released him, with the biggest smile I'd worn in several months. I decided then and there that this would be an annual trip.

Since that spring day in 1972 I have returned to Mitchell Creek each year. It has gotten only better since I've been able to make the trip with my son, my daughter, and two of my grandsons. With a third grandson not quite two years old and a granddaughter recently born, the legacy will grow. I hope they will enjoy the bottom hole and come to understand the treasure of fishing along the family legacy trail.

My father, who served in the Navy in World War II in the South Pacific, told me that fishing reconnected him with the world, and that being on a trout stream was the best sanity check a man could ask for. I know that a fly rod, that same stream, and enough time allowed me to reconnect with the world. And it was there that I saw the tears of reconciliation roll down my son's face after he returned from the horror that is Afghanistan. It is my one true hope that none of my grandchildren will need to turn to the water as a saving grace—that they are able to enjoy the truth, pleasure, and beauty of the free stone water for what it is: LIFE.

At sixty-six years of age, I am thankful that the bottom hole is at the end of the journey and close to the road. I will inevitably be forced to fish less and less of the two-mile stretch of Mitchell Creek, but I know that I will be able to stay near the end and tell everyone who asks that there are no fish there because it is so close to the road. After all, every family legacy needs a little misdirection and intrigue.

*Duane grew up in the Colorado Mountains at a D&RGW railroad station on the top of Tennessee Pass at an altitude of 10,524 feet and a population of 28. His youth was spent fishing the small streams and beaver ponds in the area, as well as the headwaters of both the Arkansas and Eagle Rivers. Fly fishing has been a constant reflective point in his life and continues today. A Vietnam veteran, in 2012 he co-founded and leads the Platte Rivers chapter of Project Healing Waters Fly Fishing, which serves veteran, disabled, and active-duty military personnel in Southeastern Wyoming and Northern Colorado. This is his first published essay.*

# Pigeon River

## Thomas Ford Conlan

*Insanity: doing the same thing over and*
*over again and expecting different results.*
*—Albert Einstein*

Branches scraped the pickup as Doc pulled off the gravel road onto a narrow two track while daylight waned on a muggy summer evening. Parked by a gate hidden from the road, we sat on the tailgate, pulled on our waders, and doped up against the mosquitos. We had a mile-and-a-half hike in to the old Hemingway cabin, where Doc said, "We have permission to fish here." But he had no key to the iron gate.

The path wound through heavy woods. Doc and I are the same size but I sweated, struggling to keep up with his long and agile strides. The woods opened up to an abandoned farm field. I looked down to avoid a puddle in a depression and noticed the sign of a bear paw in the mud. The path closed up again through tight cedar and pines, finally curving down a shallow grade to green grass, and the small stone cabin nestled a few feet from the banks of the Pigeon River.

Doc lit up a smoke. I sat on an old wooden bench by the river and tied on an Adams while we waited for the sun to drop just a touch more. The Adams is a dry fly, a mixture of gray wool and red feathers hiding a tiny number six hook. Local legend leads us to believe that a certain Judge Adams, a dedicated fly fisherman, wound this fly for a river in Northern Michigan back in the 1920s. The evening sky turned a golden pink. The cedar waxwings traded up and down the river, a good sign.

Doc and I most always split up and we did again that night as Doc said, "There's a nice hole around that corner, why don't you wade downstream?" I nodded in concurrence, knowing he wanted to fish a good hole lying around the bend just upstream.

I slid into the water right in front of the cabin and loosened up with a few air casts, which always drives Doc nuts. He generally just waits, smokes, takes one back cast, and drops the fly gently on the water. Nonetheless, I lay the line out across the river and a twelve-inch brookie took the fly. I landed him in long grass by the cabin, and watched in recurrent wonder, as I released the hook, the fish wiggled, and swam away.

Doc, no doubt wishing he'd chosen downstream, lit another smoke and watched as I carefully waded across the river and worked my way down to the first gentle bend. I stopped above a nice riffle current to get my bearings and balance on the rocky river bottom.

I blew on the fly to dry it out. Taking the rod back, I anticipated a second trout with my second cast. Concentrating on the surface of the water where I believed a trout would rise, I started to bring my rod forward. My reverie was ended abruptly by the unyielding tug of my rod tip bending backwards. The hook of the Adams stuck in the branches of a swamp alder hanging off the bank twenty feet behind me. Frustrated, I shrugged. "Aw, fuck."

Clumsily, I waded back up the river, reached up to break off the offending alder branch, and retrieved my tangled line and fly. Pissed off because I probably messed up the hole, it took me a few minutes to straighten out the line, and let the anger wear off. I worked my way back downstream to cast to the riffle again. I took a deep breath and let it out slowly. I planned two air casts before landing the fly on the third, right where a trout continued to rise. I pulled the rod back, and as I began forward, a shower of floating fly line and leader fell around my shoulders. The hook was gone.

My Adams, lost in the alder, again.

Not one to be easily defeated, I reeled in the line, eased over to sit on the bank, and lit up a Rum Crook to fight the bugs. After taking a few slow puffs on the cheap cigar, I inspected the line and leader. Both looked fine. I reached into my box to find a replacement for the lost Adams, wiped the sweat from my eyes, put on my crooked reading glasses, and tied on a new fly.

Pleased with myself and rested, I eased back out into the current. I figured the time taken tying on the new fly had let the hole rest, too. I found my balance in the stream, and with fresh vigor, prepared to cast.

Just as I raised my rod, Doc called out from the far bank. "Tom, either you're

going to have to use less line, or move to a different spot, or you're going to catch that fly in the same fuckin' tree."

I looked up, paused a moment, and replied, "You calling me stupid?"

We got a good laugh, one of those bellyaching, relaxing laughs that lasts a lifetime.

I ended up missing that hole but caught another small rainbow farther downstream. The moon hid behind the clouds. As dark and quiet enveloped the valley, I noticed a foul smell and rustling in the bushes on shore. I remembered the bear tracks, and waded back upstream, urgently.

Doc waited at the cabin. He had landed two big brown trout on the upstream bend. He said, "It's after midnight, let's hit it." We hiked back out to the truck and peeled off our waders.

Doc headed the pickup back west across the Sturgeon River into the town of Wolverine. Disappointment mounted when we found Rocky's Roadhouse closed on this weeknight. A few miles south on Highway 27 we found another bar, interestingly named "The Old Twenty-Seven." We bellied up and ordered rum and Cokes, and burgers. The place looked empty except for us and the older lady who set up the drinks. We figured she owned the place. A young guy walked through a swing door and delivered the burgers, commenting, "She's my mom."

Doc was preoccupied telling the lady the night's fishing story for the first time. He got a good laugh from the lady. Her son, listening in, also smiled at the punch line. I cringed a bit and grinned, the first of many times I would be embarrassed by Doc's telling of this tale.

The son pulled off his apron and plugged in the karaoke machine in the corner. Doc and I finished our burgers to the sound of the son, singing the lonesome strains of "Feelings," while his mother cried.

Doc asks, "Hey, you can sing and play, why don't you give it a try?"

Calmly, I replied, "You calling me stupid?"


*Thomas Ford Conlan lives, writes, fishes, and tends his grape vines in the highlands of Northern Michigan. He has captained a Coast Guard Cutter, sailed the world's lakes and oceans, and now searches for elusive brook trout because he loves the streams where they live. His favorite haunts include the Wild and Scenic Jordan; the West Branch of the Escanaba; the Pigeon, Sturgeon, and Black in Michigan; and Spearfish Creek in the Black Hills. Tom's work has appeared in* Vine Leaves Literary Journal, *the print anthology* Puppy Love, *and* TulipTree Review. *His work was chosen as a finalist for the Annie Dillard Prize in the Bellingham Review. Tom holds an MFA from Queens University of Charlotte, and a Master of Science from the U.S. Naval Postgraduate School in Monterrey, California.*

# Go Fish!

## Scott Scheffey

Go Fish!: A rudimentary but classic card game requiring little skill and even less thought. Yet, it provided an escape from whatever might concern this eight-year-old boy. As a kid I'd yell, "GO FISH!" to Mike, a guy who always had my back growing up: bullies, being dumped by a girl, breaking something—he was there. He was my best friend; still is fifty-one years later. I love my brother.

"Go Fish!" We'd laugh as each declaration became louder, more animated, sometimes physical. "I'm telling Mom!" I'd scream, as nuggies bounced off my head. I never told Mom, only because I knew a cherry belly would ensue if I did.

With card game complete, we'd hang out in the family room preoccupied with the latest issue of *Boys Life* or *Ranger Rick*: Mike reading, me cutting out ads related to military schools. I didn't want my parents remembering their threats to send me to one, and if they did remember I sure as hell didn't want them having easy access to a phone number. All the while black and white images of Vietnam, narrated by Walter Cronkite, leapt from our only television each night, and although aware, I paid little attention. Why would I? I had nothing in common with those men scrambling over severed trees, navigating dense jungles, screaming over the thwump, thwump, thwump as dozens of helicopters hovered overhead darkening the sky. Not a concern for this eight-year-old boy. Their battleground was somewhere else, the real deal, unlike my make-believe G.I. Joe battles.

Growing up in a small Pennsylvania neighborhood meant gathering up your buddies for a day of fun in the sun to play Army. Hmm . . . Army, fun, and sun. Not something anyone who's been through any military branch's basic training course would say in a single breath. Some of us boys used souvenir rifles and hats bought during a school fieldtrip to Gettysburg. Others had cooler stuff obtained from fathers and grandfathers who'd served in World War II and Korea. We were an ominous presence, so we thought. Most likely we were an annoyance to neighbors as we ran through yards screaming, falling, shooting cap guns, and throwing dirt clod grenades at the sides of houses and each other. An occasional rock in a dirt clod made a thunderous sound against aluminum siding, sending anyone in close proximity falling to the ground, simulating a casualty. Falling too slowly (you had fifteen seconds for your theatrical death performance) or refusing to do so meant a barrage of grenades rained down on you, guaranteeing you left the battlefield bruised, bloodied, and generally feeling like shit.

It's a little easier, as a kid, to turn your back on bad childhood experiences and move on. To this day I recall many bad personal decisions, embarrassments, and mistakes. My parents always said I had to learn the hard way. Still, I moved forward in a positive direction joining a local fire department as a teen, and eventually enlisting in the Air Force, becoming a security policeman in what's now known as the Security Forces.

Twenty-three years later I retired, my head filled with recollections of close friends, experiences, and locations around the globe. Most memories are good, but it's the not so good memories that haunt me. My counselor refers to those not so good memories as "yukky thoughts."

When a Blackhawk, with its blades methodically thwumping, powered by two General Electric T700 engines, tears into another Blackhawk, there isn't much left on the desert floor. Analyze that counterintuitive dilemma of physics and you'll walk away pretty sure that it didn't matter if both helicopters were moving or one was standing still. Twelve men died.

Yukky experiences burn indelible yukky thoughts into the brain. They make a person think and do strange things. For me it was withdrawing from everything. My favorite comedy shows weren't funny; colors were still colors only drab; being a volunteer firefighter was no longer exciting, but rather, burdensome. Deep thinking about my existence consumed me. At first yukky thoughts leapt at me a few days a month. Eventually they were there every day. I could be driving and find myself so preoccupied with those thoughts that I had no idea how I got from point A to point B. Was I speeding? Did I hit something? I didn't know. Time had passed as had distance.

Nights brought no relief as dreams became nightmares so intense I felt as if I'd spent several hours at the gym using every piece of strength and cardio equipment. Vomiting and crapping made me feel better. I don't know why.

Eventually I decided taking control of my existence needed immediate attention. I knew yukky thoughts had to stop. I needed to stop . . . forever.

The coolness of a glass pressed to your lips as a mixture of sweet and slightly sour orange juice fills your mouth at breakfast. Fleeting crisp notes of fall bite your nose. Wind swooshing past your ear transporting a thump-a-da, thump-a-da sound from a distant train. A mare, standing in green prairie grass whinnying for her mate. Is today the last your senses conclude their collective efforts to keep you cognizant of life?

No one knows when, how, where their time will come. I didn't know, but I tried to force God's hand, planning my demise. Plans went on for several days. Maybe weeks. I don't recall. I do remember thinking I must be crazy to have such thoughts. The most troubling for me was that I couldn't talk myself down. As an FBI-trained hostage negotiator I was able to communicate with others in distress: an armed and intoxicated Vietnam vet who wanted his mental pain from being a tunnel rat to end; the NCO who had a knife in one hand, his infant daughter in the other. How was it I helped them understand tomorrow held hope, and brought a tense, dangerous situation to a successful resolution, yet I couldn't make myself understand what I preached?

Suicidal thoughts parallel addiction. An addict struggles to control cravings for more of what they want or need. A person with suicidal ideations struggles to control yukky thoughts. Both need intervention along with love, support, and understanding from family, friends, and support organizations.

My intervention came from Dale, a neighbor. "Go fish," he proclaimed one day. He said it matter of factly. Not with as much gusto as I had said those words forty-three years earlier, but with enough enthusiasm that I asked what he meant.

Dale, several years older than me, his hair and close-cut beard white with wisdom, reminded me of Santa Clause. Jolly demeanor, eyes sparkling, not chubby though. He always had something positive to say. He greeted me cheerfully as I stepped out of my house that day. "Hello, Scott, how the heck are you, young man?"

I replied with my usual "Howdy" and watched as he placed fishing rods, waders, and other gear into the bed of his pickup truck. I walked across the street and watched Dale continue packing. I didn't say much as it appeared his attention was focused on fishing line gathered around his feet and the piece of fuzz attached to the end of the line. My eyes studied that fuzz. *Is that cat hair?*

Dale didn't notice my intent look, and continued his mental checklist and packing. Occasionally he would engage me in conversation about neighbors, cutting grass, and other generalities. I would respond with just enough words to keep from having an awkward silence. This went on for several minutes until out of thin air he asked me why I didn't seem myself today. Immediately I froze as the feeling of electricity danced over my skin. It's the feeling you get when you are in an unfamiliar place, late at night, and your mind whispers, *Hey what was that?* Even though nothing is there, the hair on your neck and arms straightens like soldiers called to attention.

Had I been that obvious? Today was an off day for me, not an unusual one, just off, brought on by a particular sound. Thwump, thwump, thwump. Wyoming Army Guard Blackhawks flew training missions earlier. I was locked and cocked, and those black birds were the trigger pull. Breathe slowly, concentrate, and get a good sight picture. Similar to what I was taught to do before squeezing the trigger on my M-16. Only I performed these steps after my trigger pull.

A person squints when they encounter bright light; it's a natural function of the body and you don't think about doing it. I didn't think about my mind reacting to that sound and going through those steps either. That's how I coped. My coping mechanism didn't always leave me feeling good though and today Dale noticed.

"Scott, what's up? You don't seem like your happy self."

Back to reality I snapped as I realized Dale was waiting for an answer.

I told Dale something I kept so close that only four others were privy to it. "I have PTSD. Not nearly to the extent a lot of vets experience, but it's there and I feel crummy some days."

"Well hell, Scott, go fish," Dale replied.

Before I could explain that I hadn't fished in decades, or that I had no idea how to use those strange-looking fishing poles or tiny balls of cat hair in his hands, Dale continued to go in-depth about fly fishing. I learned Dale was preparing for a Project Healing Waters Fly Fishing outing.

Although in a hurry to head out, Dale told me enough about fly fishing that I was hooked. A few weeks later we were on a pond. For three hours I had a blast not catching fish. It didn't matter though; my brain was engaged so deep that yukky thoughts never had a chance to open the door into my head.

That was mid-September and a few weeks later I stepped into my first Project Healing Waters gathering. Immediately I was approached by several members, each with a smile on their face. Not what I expected from vets with physical and emotional issues. I knew I belonged.

Over the next several months I built my first fly rod, provided by Project Healing Waters Fly Fishing. I had great teachers there and I guess they saw potential. I was asked to build another fly rod to enter into their national competition. Whether I was fishing, building fly rods, or tying flies (I discovered you don't use cat hair), the end of the day was the same: no yukky thoughts.

Almost a year and several purchases of fly rods, flies, and equipment later, I find myself happier, physically healthier, and understood more deeply by my wife, Nancy. She understands I am broken but on the mend. Perhaps I don't need seven fly rods, but she understands. Fly fishing changed me—she understands. And now she knows I own more than two fly rods. I hope she understands.

As I step over birch trees recently felled by beavers, a barely noticeable breeze wafts hints of decaying grass from their pond and excites all of my senses. At the water's edge I sweep aside a light coating of algae, watching the still dirty surface for signs of life. The wait isn't long; insects begin to appear over, around, and under shallow water. Some gently touch down, while others glide from a muddy bottom bounded by decaying logs partially hidden by the murky water. Those insects guide me in my selection of the perfect flies for today's escape.

Capturing the magic of nature by enticing a perch or brookie onto my line takes me back to that eight-year-old boy. A boy whose childhood friends are there with me for a fleeting moment. Eventually the sun fades away as do Bobby, Richie, Rodney, and Johnnie. I retrace my steps out of the timber and thickets onto a dirt road. Fishing rods, waders, and other gear are packed into the bed of my pickup truck.

I focus on fishing line gathered around my feet and the piece of fuzz attached to the end. Several frustrating minutes go by and more line becomes entangled around the only wild plant, Indian paintbrush, within several yards. I decide my yellow line and the orange-red flower balance each other and gather both into a ball, tossing rod, line, and plant into my truck. I smile because even a tangled line engaged my brain, leaving no room for yukky thoughts.

*Scott Scheffey hails from Pennsylvania and followed his father's footsteps, enlisting in the United States Air Force. While writing his story, Scott researched his family's military roots, tracing them back to the Revolutionary War. During his journey Scott discovered a relative, whose battle with alcohol, after military service, ended with an early death. Scott offers a glimpse into his own military career of twenty-three years stained with several disturbing incidents and his personal struggle with Post-Traumatic Stress Disorder. Combining fly fishing and writing, he found a release from his demons. Scott hopes by sharing his story you appreciate that life is awesome, worth living to its fullest and pursuing all your passions. Believe it, create it, go and do it!*

# Return and Release

## V. B. Puzick

Ten miles south of the small town of Deckers, Colorado, Highway 67 rounds a long curve at the top of a ridge. The view at the top is not uncommon in Colorado: the long and broad flat plateau stretches out, populated with pines and aspen trees while off in the distance rocky peaks capture the early morning sun. At the far end of the curve, the highway begins to descend and for the next ten miles you wind your way down sharp hairpin turns and milder, sweeping curves to the tailwaters out of Cheesman Reservoir and the South Platte River below Deckers.

This stretch of the South Platte established itself as one of the premiere fisheries in Colorado after the Cheesman Dam was finished in 1905. Cheesman Canyon became catch-and-release waters in 1976, the first of such waters in the state, and three years later

it was designated as a Wild Trout River. The Canyon holds trophy brown and cutthroat trout while downstream, the South Platte provides its own challenges for fly fishermen.

In the late 1960s, we would load my dad's blue-bodied, wood-paneled station wagon with our gear and head to Deckers and this renowned river, only an hour or so from our home, and we would fish. My brother, sometimes my sister, and I would try our best with the spinning rod and reel. Phil, at sixteen years old, would do better than the rest of us. The fishing contests were usually fought between him and my dad. At ten years old, I didn't stand much of a chance. I was sort of the pesky little brother along for the ride, doing my best not to get tangled or to stand behind my dad when he made his cast. The banks of that river, though, with the sound of the water, the hawks riding currents overhead, and the occasional deer spotted on the surrounding hills made for deep-rooted memories.

In 1969 that scene changed. In the fall, my brother headed off to Colorado State University. Not long after that, on my walk home from North Junior High and a half block away from our house on Nevada Avenue, I watched my father pull that same Ford station wagon away from the curb in front of our house. We waved. He had been given the alcoholic's final ultimatum from my mother: quit drinking or leave. Over the next six years, I would see my father a handful of times, some weekends here and there when he made it back into town. After I graduated from high school, our contact virtually ended.

I moved away from Colorado Springs, pursued my own degree at Colorado State, and then moved even farther away. I progressed into my own alcoholism and drug use. Addiction is insidious. I moved farther away from those foundational things that make me who I am. I stopped fishing. I stopped backpacking. Stopped doing much at all in the way of going to the outdoors, to the mountains. My life became smaller. Self-contained and self-absorbed. Burned out.

And then something happened. I got sober. And after my first year of sobriety, I made the drive back to Colorado from California to try to clean up the relationship I had with my dad, now in a nursing home due to a stroke that left him paralyzed on his right side and unable to speak other than minimal utterances of "yeah" or "no" along with a shake of his head. Our "conversation" at the nursing home basically consisted of my telling him a little about my job but mostly about getting sober. Neither one of us was particularly religious, but when I mentioned my sobriety, my father moved his left hand and pointed upward. "God." I laughed a little bit and said, "Yeah, that's right!"

My dad died not long after that. We didn't have much of a chance to clear any of the past, to talk as two men rather than solely as a father and son. We didn't get another chance to fish together. And as it happens, we were framed in the way we used to be. I'd be that ten-year-old boy struggling to get his fly on the water and frustrating the man upstream who was fighting his own battles.

During the first few years of my recovery, I worked on the forgiveness that would need to happen if there was any chance of healing the relationship between my dad and me. Even though he had died, the way that I related to my father and how I viewed our relationship, continued on. For years into my recovery process, I looked at that relationship the best way that I could, turning it in my mind to view it from this angle and that. I was twelve when he left, twenty-eight when he died, and two years sober when I began to forgive. Began.

It took me a long time to fish again after I moved back to Colorado, to return to the mountains for reasons other than hiking. Recovery is like that, taking its own sweet time around long sweeping curves, sometimes dropping into a valley, and then pulling long grades back up to the top of the ridge before you recover who you were before addiction, and recover those things that matter in your life.

In 2002, the Deckers area was nearly burned out due to the Hayman Fire. Ironically, a forest ranger, angry at being jilted by her ex-husband, started the fire when she decided to burn a letter she received from him. The winds, strong enough to actually inspire a fire ban in the Colorado mountains, lifted that burning paper and dropped it into the surrounding trees. Nearly 138,000 acres later—after spreading over ridges and dipping into valleys—that fire was finally put down by fire fighters.

But the damage was done. The South Platte River was severely impacted. Of course, the forest fires caused ash to be washed down into the water with the rains in the fall and, later, the spring runoff from the winter snows. With nothing to hold down any topsoil or the pea-sized Pike's Peak granite of these hillsides, the erosion further decimated the river. Sediment, carried into the waters of smaller streams feeding the South Platte, filled the fishing holes and reshaped the river. Bug life nearly disappeared—and with that loss, the fish population was impacted.

In 2009, my first summer of fly fishing, I decided to drive up to Deckers—pretty much unaware of, or inattentive to, the dismal conditions and damage done to the fishery. The drive there was both exhilarating and disheartening. Although I was just a small boy when I rode with my father to this river, the road felt familiar. Not the kind of familiarity of "there's a cool view around this next corner," but a more visceral kind of memory. An emotional memory.

And my memories were confounded. I recalled the excitement of the descent into Deckers and the prospect of fishing with my dad and my brother. I remembered the morning air, crisp with the smell of pine and of river. And I held the memories of a distant father, fishing upstream and then gone.

The hills now along that stretch of Highway 67 have skeletal pine trees populating the hillsides. It stuns me, takes my breath away, each curve offering a different view of a distant hillside. It's always a surreal sight, once-green forests of Ponderosa Pine and Douglas Fir are now black trunks stark with charred limbs. Eventually groundcover will begin to crop up here and there over the hills. Each trip, I begin to watch for aspens. Aspen trees will be the first to return to the burn areas— preceding the return of pines and signaling a deeper recovery of the area. But it's a long process. Recovery is like that.

Forgiveness is like that, too. For years I said I had forgiven my father. Forgiven him for that wave from the station wagon as if he were just going to the grocery store. Forgiven him for missing high school baseball games. For not teaching me to tie the Renegade or the Royal Coachman on the vise in the basement. I had forgiven him, at different points along the path of my own recovery, to the best of my ability.

My first times out on the tailwaters near Deckers as a fly fisherman were more of a mere walk along the river with rod in hand. I didn't really know what I was doing or have the skills to do well. The only thing I brought to the net those early trips was the excitement of being out there.

Over the next couple of summers and fall seasons, just as the ground-cover became a little more prominent on the hillsides around Deckers and the white bark of the aspens became visible, I caught a few fish. Nothing huge. Not a whole lot of them. But I had fish. Some of the fish became statements at my father. *At* him. I felt I had something to prove, something tangible to hold, to show that I had made it despite his absence.

Signs that Deckers seemed to turn the corner as a fishery became clear in 2014. Twelve years after the worst forest fire in Colorado history, Deckers' recovery appears to be at hand. For sure, the drive down into the canyon is still marked by the skeletal trees. The toothpick trunks with brittle and charred branches, barren of any needles, still silhouette the ridges, the blackened bark dark against the sky.

The recovery of the area, though, is not just about what is happening on the surface. The bug hatches have returned. The banks and bottom of the South Platte have stabilized as less sediment washes down. Big browns and beautiful rainbow trout are reproducing naturally and repopulating deep pools of its waters beyond the stocking efforts of the Division of Parks and Wildlife.

I make my way down into that valley again, past the little fly shop and grocery store that we had driven by forty-plus years ago. I head north on Highway 67, paralleling the bank of the river to find some runs I had not fished before. Past Trumbull. Past Bridge Crossing.

I park and pull on my waders and boots. The mid-morning, late-summer sun is already warm. I make my way down to the river and work my way upstream, fishing near the bank and then into some seams farther out, behind some of the larger, submerged rocks. I find a shallow run, fish it, and then cross the river to fish from the other side.

Fish are rising sporadically this September day. I make my way to a sweeping bend in the river across from a large rock jutting from the bank into the river. The flow has created a large hole on the downstream side of the rock.

I watch the water before making my first cast. Sometimes I have to slow myself down, not rush the approach to the water or force the presentation of the fly. Slow to the rhythm of the river so the cast and the drift are just part of the process. I watch the way the water cushions a little against the upstream side of the rock then flows around it. An eddy forms against the bank behind the rock. If I can get my fly on that far seam, I might stand a chance. I don't see a fish but feel he is there, feeding in that seam under the protection of the rock.

It might have been the first cast. The better story would have it be the first cast. I'm not sure if it was or not. And I am not sure if I actually saw the fish take the hopper pattern from the surface or if I just anticipated the strike and set the hook. But he is on.

And he races downstream. The line speeds off of my reel. I make my way downstream with him.

Then he turns and races upstream, my line screaming from the reel again. He tires. I retrieve some line. He turns for another downstream run. I back-step to a gravelly bar at the bank of the river. Bring him in.

I admire this fish. The fight he fought. The broad expanse of his tail. The vivid color of his rainbow sides glistening, here, in this mid-day sun.

He is a beautiful fish. "Dad would be proud. He'd like this fish." And I realize that I didn't catch this fish to prove anything to my dad. I didn't catch this fish *at* him.

Recovery is like that.

To truly forgive my father, I had to go deeper. I couldn't remain at the surface of the skeletal trees and burned out groundcover. It wasn't merely about missed baseball games or untied flies. It wasn't his wave from the station wagon. I had to go deeper, to the roots. What was lost was the relationship between a father and his son. I had to acknowledge, and accept for what it was, the hurt. The loss. Forgiveness is not about expecting the other person to change in order to be forgiven. He is dead; there is no changing him. It's not about trying to paint a different picture of what the truth of the past actually was. There is no going back. Would I have wanted a different relationship with my father? Absolutely. But to hold to the phantom image of a different, unattainable relationship made it impossible to forgive the man for the relationship that was.

I take the trout from the net. Admire him one last time. His length. His color. Feel his weight in my hand as I submerge him back into the river.

And let him go.

*V. B. (Vince) Puzick is a Colorado native. Having spent much of his childhood and adolescence fishing, hiking, and backpacking in the Colorado mountains, he feels most at home and most connected to the world when he is somewhere in thin, pine-scented air with a river nearby. As a recovering alcoholic, he turns to the natural world as a foundation of his recovery and to rejuvenate his spirit. He shares long roadtrips and fishes winding stretches of Colorado's small streams with his love, Jannetta, and his daughter, Jessica. He lives and writes in Colorado Springs.*

# Starting Over

## Bryan Lally

From the time I was thirteen years old I successfully avoided fishing. My aversion was tied to my preteen years, when a day on the water meant all my patience and anticipation would be rewarded with empty-handed frustration

My father didn't fish so I knew nothing about the sport, but I decided that for my ninth birthday I wanted a rod and reel. Dad got me a kid-sized Zebco, which I prized as much as my bike. There weren't many fishable waters near my hometown in the Maryland suburbs of Washington, D.C., so the best opportunities came on those family vacations that took us near water, any water. If we were at the beach, I'd go out after dinner, stand in the sand as I tied on a random lure, then cast out as far as I could, which was often not even beyond the break. The only fish I ever saw was a dead pufferfish that washed up after a storm.

One year we visited Yosemite National Park and I fished a beautiful little stream that was clear enough for me to easily make out each smooth stone at the bottom. It was also clear enough for me to make out some nice-sized trout swimming past my bait without hesitation.

The final straw came on a Cub Scout father-son fishing trip at the Port Tobacco River in rural Maryland. The day was cold and windy with off-and-on drizzle, making the murky gray river even more dismal. We fished off a creaky old dock that was slowly falling into the river. The other Scouts and I stood there, mostly in silence, none of us wanting to sound like a baby by complaining about how miserable we were. No one got even a nibble and the only excitement came when I was backing away from the edge of the dock and a couple planks gave way. I fell backward into the gap, but somehow my pants and jacket got snagged on the way down. I hung there like a hammock until my father pulled me out. After that I swore off fishing, my career ended with a perfect record of zero fish caught.

For thirty-five years I kept my vow of abstinence, even after moving to Portland, Oregon, which is a haven for fly fishing. Then one day my friend Greg, a longtime fly fisherman, started talking about something he recently discovered called "tenkara." He told me it's a traditional Japanese fly fishing method for catching the smaller trout that inhabit mountain streams.

He invited me to join him in trying tenkara up on Mount Hood, a majestic, glacier-topped peak that dominates the eastern skyline of Portland. The more he talked about it, the more it pulled at me. But the lessons of my youth were deeply rooted.

He described the tenkara equipment—there's no reel, just a rod and line—it's basically a string on a stick. That didn't help his case. If I couldn't catch anything with real fishing equipment, how could I expect to do any better with some kind of Huckleberry Finn rig? But Greg is very persuasive when he's enthusiastic about something and he was clearly excited about tenkara. I fell for the pitch and agreed to go.

We headed up to the Salmon River, which is fed by springs and snowmelt at the higher elevations of Mount Hood. At the area where we set up the river is about sixty feet wide, and aside from the occasional eddy, runs no deeper than a few feet, with a mild current. The banks are studded with rocks that range from pebbles to boulders. Douglas fir, red cedar, and larch trees spread shade out to the water's edge. The water is clear and once the sun climbs over the ridge, the surface shimmers from end to end. All you can hear out there is the chirping of birds and the steady rush of water over rock.

We took turns with the tenkara rod, keeping an eye on the overhanging branches, making short casts out into the riffle, letting the current carry the fly into the calm water just beyond. Once we got going, my opinion turned from doubting the simple equipment to respecting it. The telescoping carbon fiber rod extends out to eleven feet, so flexible you could practically bend it in half. Attached to the end of the pole is a ten-foot braided lead with a five-foot tippet. At the end of the tippet is the fly, in this case one that looked like a flying ant. With a little practice I was able to land the fly more or less where I wanted it.

After a few casts, my eyes adjusted to the glittering surface, allowing me to follow the fly as it floated along. Suddenly there was a little splash, and the pole started wiggling in my hand. Greg yelled, "Fish on!" My brain caught fire instantly. "Keep the tip up!" he said. "Don't let the line go slack!" I followed his directions unconsciously, gradually pulling the fish closer to shore. Greg grabbed the lead and a rainbow trout popped out of the water. It was just six inches long, but it might as well have been a marlin. At age forty-eight I'd caught my first fish.

Over the course of the next few hours I also caught my second, third, and fourth fish. None of them would be considered a prize to the average fisherman, but it didn't matter. I wouldn't have kept them anyway. Even when I was a kid, my aim was never to fish for a meal or a trophy; the victory was in making the catch. To kill the fish would just be rubbing it in.

Back home, flush with success, I felt confident enough to encourage my nine-year-old son to join me for a return trip to the mountain. Within a few weeks I'd bought a tenkara rod of my own and he and I were on the Salmon

River. My boy caught on quickly, and aside from getting tangled in the trees, he handled the rod pretty well. He even landed a cutthroat, which thrilled me almost as much as it did him.

Now we each have our own rods and we are regulars at the streams and small rivers that flow down Mount Hood. My son has started talking about learning how to use a fly reel, so it probably won't be long before he wants to head out to the coastal rivers to take on the salmon and steelhead that run there. He may even convince me to join him, but for now I am content with my string on a stick.

*Bryan Lally is a freelance writer and reporter. His previous work has appeared in the Yellow Chair Review and Shotgun Honey. He and his family live in Portland, Oregon.*

# With a Perfect Drift

## Ken McCoy

As I stepped into the cool waters of the river, a few of our guide's words kept resonating in my head: "the river will not judge you." This river didn't know who I was, where I came from, or why I was here. It didn't know my past and certainly would never know my future. My future, as far as I or the river knew, was somewhere downstream, a long way downstream. My future had no picture in my head, it played no reel. Downstream, like my future, was an impossibility to comprehend. My past I could comprehend. That had pictures. Not the best pictures. My past had many tapes that continually played over and over again in my head like a home movie or a low-budget documentary with only me commentating. Sometimes there was video, other times only darkness, but there was always a commentator. *You're not good enough. You can't do it. Something is wrong with you.*

We had met our guide, Christopher, at the shop around 7:30 earlier that morning. Not sure why we didn't get an afternoon trip. I couldn't remember the last time I slept well. The rest of the small mountain town was still waking up but this fly shop was full of people. The lady at the front desk checked us in, confirming our reservation and taking the remainder of the price of the trip, less the deposit we had already put down. She checked us out with a couple of out-of-state fishing licenses. After running my credit card at the shop, we were introduced to our guide. He was pretty much exactly what I had envisioned a fly fishing guide in the Rockies to be: thin, beard, sporting a trucker hat, and just enough camo to know he was an outdoor guy. His waders were plenty worn, showing he obviously spent plenty of time in them. His cap was spotted with a number of different fly patterns. The only one I recognized looked like some sort of red worm.

Christopher escorted us through the gear-packed shop where he asked for our shoe sizes and found a couple pairs of waders that he thought would work. There appeared to be several other trips going out that same morning as the wader area was crowded with eager fishermen and guides pretending not to be impatient. As Dad and I were trying on our waders and boots, Christopher asked several probing questions in an attempt to get to know us a little. He was feeling out our experience level with fishing, fly fishing in particular. Being from Missouri, my dad and I spent a couple of times each summer fishing for bass; this was my first attempt at catching trout. I believe my dad had fly fished a couple of times over the years, possibly when I was too young and uninterested to go along, possibly when I was overseas. I couldn't pinpoint any of those trips and he didn't mention anything to Christopher during our brief conversation. As we headed out the back door of the shop after suiting up, Christopher explained that we would be fishing tailwater, which, based on his description, was the portion of the river directly downstream from a dam. The thought of standing below a dam and listening to its roar gave me anxiety. It was obvious the amount of knowledge that Christopher had of his craft and he wasn't afraid to let us know. I had just met the guy but he seemed like an arrogant prick.

"The river will not judge you." I'm sure this was Christopher's way of telling us we were going to be terrible and he couldn't wait to fish for himself. He explained to us that we weren't casting to fish where our flies landed, but rather, downstream where our flies would float. He called it the "drift." If we got the drift right, we'd be sure to catch fish. He also said that by the time we actually got a strike, several fish would have seen and disregarded our flies. I guess I never realized how particular trout were. Honestly, I'm not sure I had ever thought about it. My dad had told me something about trying to change people when I was younger. "Daniel," he said, "some things in life just won't change and there's nothing you can do about it, no matter how hard you try." Later that morning, as I found myself attempting to will those fish into striking, my dad's words came back to me.

The river was dotted with large boulders like an old paved road that had been patched numerous times after countless punishing winters, each boulder showing just enough of its self to announce its presence in the water and give the occasional bird or two a place to rest its wings. During the drive from the fly shop, Christopher had explained that trout will hang out behind these large rocks. He went on to explain that trout typically like to find a place in the river that is relatively calm but close to faster water.

This strategy allows the fish to conserve energy and have easy access to a floating, conveyer belt buffet of aquatic insects. "Trout are lazy," he said. We would, of course, be targeting these areas by casting our flies upstream to the calmer water and allowing the bait to be carried along with the other bugs and be presented to the trout as a tasty buffet option. *You aren't good enough.*

The river's flow didn't seem fast as we had approached but as I began to wade out I could feel the power of the water as I struggled to find my footing on the slick rocks submerged at the bottom. The force of the water squeezed the waders against my legs and it felt as if gravity had increased below my waist. Back at home, life was the water and I was the waders being overwhelmed by the surrounding pressure. Over eight hundred miles away, everything seemed like a slick rock just waiting to throw off my balance and leave me soaking wet. They didn't understand me. I wanted to punch every one of them in their stupid, ignorant faces. *You don't fit in.*

I stopped twenty feet or so out at a spot I could get my balance. Christopher was just downstream with my dad and I could see him pointing to the location in the river that he wanted my dad to cast. A wave of anxiety came rushing down the river and hit me full force. *You can't do this. Just run away. Have a glass of whiskey.*

I froze, just standing in the middle of the river with a hypnotized stare at the ripples of water just upstream from me. The tapes were playing increasingly louder. It was noisy. What *was* I doing here? I didn't feel safe. I needed to be home, on my couch, with the television on, a beer in my hand, the lights off. That was safe. That's where I felt comfortable. I'm not certain how long I had been standing there staring at the water when I heard a whistle. With a quick duck, I snapped out of it. I clenched my rod with all my might and my hands began to tremor. Every muscle in my body tightened. I looked downstream to where Christopher and my dad were fishing. Christopher raised his arm and gave me the thumbs up and crooked his head as if to ask, "Is everything okay?" After a brief moment, I returned the thumbs up and nodded my head. I wanted to wade downstream and rip his arm right out of the socket. I turned my attention back upstream and began pulling line out of the reel. *Give up now.*

The cast Christopher had taught us on the bank was actually pretty simple. I had seen plenty of people fly fishing on TV and that looked extremely difficult but what Christopher had shown us was nothing like what I had seen before. He used the terms "pick up" and "lay down." I let the flies and strike indicator float downstream to my right so that the line was taut. At that point I raised my arm high into the air, turning the reel toward me so that I could see its face, as Christopher had instructed us. I then pushed my arm forward and upstream to my left, flicking my wrist at the very end, again, as Christopher had instructed. My line piled up in front of me. I could feel my stomach begin to knot. *You can't do this.*

Flicking my rod tip back and forth I allowed the line to float back down stream again. With a little more force and a greater downward motion, this cast proved to be more successful and my line ended in a relatively straight line directly to my left. The line quickly began floating downstream and directly toward my legs. Anger swelled up in me from deep under the surface of the water. *You're useless.*

I managed to get the line in front of me and allowed it to again float downstream. This time, paying more attention to where my rod tip stopped, I managed a decent cast both upstream and out in front of me, essentially at my ten o'clock. *Maybe you can do this.*

I watched my strike indicator float downstream just this side of the rock that Christopher had instructed me to aim for. It wasn't a perfect drift but it was certainly better than all of my previous attempts. I waited a few seconds at the end of the drift to allow my flies to swing out. I raised my arm high again in preparation of my next cast. I managed to land it in the same spot but with a little less grace and the line wasn't as straight. As I eyed my pink strike indicator from left to right, I saw Christopher coming upstream toward me. "You're doing great," he said in a quiet voice. "Now let's see if we can improve that drift and get a fish on."

He reached for my rod and I handed it to him. I could feel my body beginning to tense up. Anxiety and anger were starting to consume me again. I focused briefly on the location where I was going to cast and then gave all of my attention to Christopher's instruction, in particular the mechanics of his casting arm. I felt my body start to relax as he explained the proper casting technique again along with some additional tricks for managing the line after the cast. This he called mending. It all seemed pretty straightforward. It definitely was a lot of information to soak in but as my brain put all of the pieces together, it began to make sense. Line taut downstream, arm high, down and forward with force and a flick, then mend.

After countless casts and a few additional pointers from Christopher, I believe I saw my strike indicator dunk underwater. If there had been a fish there, it was long gone by the time my brain realized what was happening, thus sending a message to my arm to set the hook. My reaction time just wasn't as good as it had been a few years ago. I didn't want to miss another and became fascinated with the drift of the strike indicator as it floated from my ten o'clock downstream to my right. Floating high on the water it projected to me the riffles, slow spots, whirls, and waves of the river. Like a three-dimensional EKG, my strike indicator diligently reporting the heartbeat of the river. I'm not sure I blinked. As the indicator reached the end of each run, I'd give my line a quick jerk and then prepare my line for the next cast. Again I'd watch intently as the strike indicator floated down past me. Time had stopped. Only the river and I existed in that moment. The only movement was the water flowing downstream and my arm becoming increasingly comfortable with each cast. I felt a breeze hit the back of my neck. The roar of the dam just upstream from me had seemingly stopped. I watched a leaf land near my strike indicator, joining it for a synchronized drift down the river. I looked down past them both and saw my dad fighting a fish, Christopher by his side with his net in hand, the rod bent into a perfect arch. The sun was high in the sky and light bounced off the water causing tiny rainbows in the mist just above the white water that smashed into the boulders. I could still feel the cool water squeezing my calves as I stood there thinking about nothing, still not blinking.

I'm not certain how long I had been standing there, my flies holding downstream causing a small wake around the strike indicator, when Christopher appeared a couple arm lengths downstream from me. "Now let's get you one, buddy," he said.

My dad had apparently caught two nice rainbows and a small brown. Where had I been when all of this was going on? I had a fleeting feeling of confusion but felt remarkably at ease. Christopher told me to reel in my line. We were relocating to a spot just downstream from where my dad was having luck. Leapfrogging, he called it. I didn't mind. It made sense given I hadn't been catching anything after fishing that same spot for . . . wait, how long had I been fishing that spot? I gave my casting location a glance over my shoulder, followed by a nod as if to say "Thank you," as we reached the bank and began down the trail. As we passed my dad, I gave him a thumbs-up and a smile. Christopher tossed a bottle of water back to me and I wasted no time getting in a few big chugs as we walked. This was working out to be a damn fine day. After a few hundred yards, Christopher stopped and squatted down, eyeing the water in front of him. He waved me over. He explained to me what he was seeing of the water, where the fish would be holding, and how to best go about fishing for them. I was ready. Christopher quickly stopped me. He wanted to change out my flies. "I've fished this spot a ton of times. I don't what it is, probably something on the floor of the river, but I always slay them with worm patterns. Doesn't matter what time of year or what else is working in other places. I'm putting on a Squirmy Wormy as your lead fly and a Hot Head Soft Hackle Sow Bug about eighteen inches below that on a smaller tippet." Or at least, that's what I think he said. I will admit, I wasn't giving him 100 percent of my attention. I wanted to get back in that water as quickly as possible. The longer I stood along the bank the more I missed that feeling of absolute serenity.

Christopher finished and I slowly began wading out to the spot he pointed out. This time I was less concerned with my cast and was eager to see what a fish felt like on the other end of my fly rod. Besides, isn't that the whole point—netting a fish and capturing a hero shot that you can post on whatever social media site is the latest and greatest thing? The whole social media thing is crap and simply another mechanism designed to keep semi-intelligent Americans distracted from the real travesties happening around us. First there was radio and when that wasn't enough, TV came along. TV ruled the distraction game for a long time, becoming increasingly creative at

reinventing itself to draw more and more people in while separating them from their own minds and unique ways of thinking.

I was halfway across the river by the time I realized where my mind had gone, and snapped out of it. I wasn't here to fall into the constant disgust my mind had become accustomed to. I was here to fish, to allow the flow of the river to wash all that bullshit out. Like a flood that causes the river to change course, huge amounts of water and earth cutting a new path, a better path, a more efficient path.

Yes, sometimes a house is lost, structures destroyed, lives changed forever, but great change takes great sacrifice and instead of cursing the process we should celebrate it and love the outcome, appreciate the product of the grim and unpleasant steps necessary to get there. My mind was back on track and I was ready to start casting again. With each cast I could feel the tension being released. It was as if the tension in my body was directly attached to the very tip of my line: the tippet providing a conduit to the fly line, the fly line providing a conduit to the reel, the reel passing it along to the rod, and the rod being an extension of my body, connected at my hand. With each back cast the tension traveled up from deep inside my body, down my arm, through my hand, and into the rod. With each forward cast, the tension traveled from the rod to the reel, through the fly line and out to the tippet where it would hit the first fly and explode like an invisible water balloon, right into the river. I wanted to cast every drop of tension out of my body and into that water so that it could be swept downstream and gone forever. I let go of the line from my left hand as I allowed the line to shoot forward and land softly on the water.

Mend. Strip the line slowly. Keep your rod tip up. Follow the strike indicator with your rod tip. Now start to drop the rod tip. Keep following that indicator. Mend again. My strike indicator disappeared under the water. It took a brief second for my

mind to comprehend what was happening. I lifted my rod quickly in the air. I felt a tug but nothing happened. The line went slack. I stripped line in with my left hand. BOOM! The line went tight and the rod bent over in front of me. The tug turned into a shaking, quivering, yanking force that seemed intent on taking my rod for a ride down the river.

"Let him run!" I heard Christopher yell from the bank. I let go of the line and the fish took off downstream, pulling line from the spool of the reel. It stopped. He hadn't gone

far. Keeping my rod tip high in the air, I started to reel again. The trout exploded out of the water, tumbling in midair showing his silvery sides and white bottom, diving deep as soon as he hit the water. Christopher was wading out to me with his net at the ready. Reel him. Rod tip up. Easy.

The trout would fight hard for a few moments and then sort of relax. When he wasn't pulling hard against the line, I would reel as fast as I could. My rod was bent over high in the air the entire fight. The fish would take a little and then I would take a little more. After what seemed like several minutes, Christopher was just downstream from me and had the trout in his net. I looked upstream to where my dad was standing and put my fist in the air. He returned a high thumbs up. Christopher had dislodged the fly from the corner of the trout's mouth and was bringing the netted fish to me. I dipped my hands into the water and reached into the net to pick him up. Christopher snapped a quick picture. I held the magnificent rainbow in the water, pointing upstream as Christopher had instructed. After a few seconds, the fish bolted out of my hand with a couple firm kicks of the tail. He was again at peace where he belonged.

I was at peace. As I watched that trout swim downstream and out of sight, I realized that my tape had stopped playing. The pictures were faded and almost unrecognizable. The river wasn't judging me. My present was merely surrounded by water. The longer I knelt there in the cool water, the more I realized that my present was merely temporary, as was the water, as was that beautiful rainbow, as were both my future and my past. The words, the pictures, and the tapes were washed downstream by the rivers flow, with a perfect drift.

*Ken McCoy is a Colorado native and has been fishing for trout as long as he can remember. His father put a fly rod in his hand some thirty years ago and he has never looked back. Ken is a part-time fly fishing guide based out of Estes Park. His primary quarry is trout but he will target anything that bends a rod. When he is not on the water, you will find him tying flies, writing, or chasing bits and bytes in the IT industry. Ken follows his passion of fly fishing with the loving support of his amazing wife and four beautiful daughters.*

# Fisherman's Briefcase

## Timothy O'Leary

My father's two uniforms. First, Dad the working stiff, dressed in one of three near-identical charcoal suits, always purchased on sale. "Hart Shafner Marx—best suit in the world," he'd say, brushing the shoulders and lapel before rehanging it. "Never wears out and never goes out of style." Spotless white shirt, tiny-knotted black tie, white pocket patch, and a hat to cover his buzz-cut head; a cream straw Stetson in the spring and summer, a short-brimmed wool Borsalino with a black band in the fall and winter.

And the warm-weather uniform, his fishing suit: canvas work pants covered by felt-soled rubber hip boots, a beat-up wide brimmed hat, Pendleton gold and blue plaid work shirt, and most of all I remember his creel. Dad stood in the stream with a huge straw suitcase strapped under his arm, ornate leather straps circling his shoulder and chest. This was the fisherman's briefcase, finest on the water. Thick, intricately woven yellow straw, trimmed with chocolate cowhide he patiently rubbed with Hubbard's Saddle Grease. A large nail clippers—the forerunner to today's fancy nippers—hanging from the side on a leather shoelace. Before he went fishing he'd line the creel with fresh damp grass, building a green bed for the trout he hoped to catch, then drop his cracked fly wallet inside. When he returned to the cabin I'd peek inside, anxious to discover two or three stiff and shiny red trout Mom would transform into dinner, the grass sticky-slick from their corpses.

When I'm old enough to fish my father is standing downstream, pipe clenched between his teeth, the creel protruding out his side. He yells instruction and encouragement as cruel trees reach out to snatch my leader, or I snap off hooks, wincing at the distinctive ping of fly hitting rock. When I'm most frustrated, wind whipping my line, and sure that I will never master the art of fly fishing, he's standing beside me, slowing the action, reaching into the creel to uncover an apple that he rinses in the river and hands to me. "Take a bite and maybe a fish will too." Sometimes he pulls out a hidden beer for himself, occasionally allowing me a grimaced foamy sip.

The creel holds many unexpected pleasures. A bologna sandwich, pink mystery meat encased in doughy Wonder bread and slathered with mayonnaise and yellow mustard, wrapped tight in waxed paper. When fishing was slow, he'd theatrically flip back the top of the creel as if performing a magic trick. "Presto, chango to this magic Joe's Hopper." He'd smile while extracting the fly from a wool patch.

One afternoon as we wade the Boulder River a coiled rattler screams at us, and with one swift motion Dad stomps on the snake with his big boots before it strikes. I

cower in terror, but his lack of fear is calming. He finishes off the viper with a rock, then picks it up with a stick, an action I find terrifying, revolting, and very brave. Once he's sure it's dead he puts it in the creel to transport to the cabin, where he and his buddy Tom skin it and add the rattles to the dangerous collection strung across a rafter. After that, given my irrational fear of snakes, I always peer through the square hole in the top of the creel to make sure he didn't leave a chattering guest.

By the time I'm old enough to buy my own creel, a movie called *A River Runs through It* makes fly fishing hip, and suddenly the streams are lined with Orvis-clad neophytes flailing water with expensive Sage rods, attempting to channel their inner Brad Pitt. It dawns on fly fishermen that given their exploding ranks, killing trout for food ultimately signals the demise of the sport. Catch and release becomes the fly fisherman's credo—de-barb those hooks—making the creel obsolete, to be replaced with lightweight Nike-esque high-tech fishing vests; clever tools to safely remove hooks hanging like Christmas ornaments. And the creel is relegated to become a stylish knick-knack adorning Ralph Lauren–inspired cabins.

Thirty years later when my father passes away, I dig through a basement overflowing with seven decades of stuff to discover his creel. I clean it, repair a rotted strap, and hang it on my den wall, flanking it with action shots taken on famous Montana trout streams.

Some inanimate objects absorb happiness, and because the creel exudes so many good memories, it saddens me to see other old creels discarded in junk shops and garage sales, like discarded friends. I buy them, and they line the floor and shelves of my den, now a home for abandoned fishing equipment. The oldest, purportedly handmade over two hundred years ago, came from Scotland. Another has the initials WHR burned into the leather, sometimes leaving me guessing the owner's name. A couple were handmade, others crafted in long-forgotten artisan factories. One contained a rusted reel and salmon fly probably last used during the Truman administration. But I envision them all in their prime, damp with moisture from dancing trout, repositories of laughter and joy from long-gone fishermen.

*Raised in Montana, Timothy O'Leary is an Oregon-based writer. His articles, essays, and fiction have appeared in dozens of magazines and anthologies, and he was a finalist for the 2015 Mississippi Review Prize, the Washington Square Review Fiction Prize, the Aestas Short Story Award, and the Mark Twain award for humor writing. His nonfiction book,* Warriors, Workers, Whiners & Weasels, *was published in 2006. An avid fly fisherman and environmentalist, he serves on the boards of The Freshwater Trust and The Wild Salmon Center. More information can be found at timothyolearylit.com.*

# River MASH

## T. M. Aringdale

All wars leave ripples well beyond their historical dates—not just in the lives and landscapes that survive the violence, but also within the fabric of those brave renegades who stood firmly in protest against such human folly. There are places in nature where all of these wounds and separations can be temporarily transcended, as if meandering drainages flowing from snowcapped peaks have the power to wash away the emotional/moral/intellectual grip of war, revealing the inner dignity and resilience of *Homo sapiens*. The Wounded Warriors veteran support group has a program that exposes PTSD-stricken ex-soldiers to the therapeutic effects of fly fishing. This life-affirming work opens hearts on the banks of scenic rivers, churning the clinging past into a freer present, allowing a fresh perspective to emerge that can overcome the cycling dictates of haunting memories.

One bright May morning on the Big Thompson—a river I regard as my personal backyard fishery—I chanced upon a Vietnam veteran from New Mexico who had just caught a giant German brown on a very tiny sow bug. He and I had been eyeing each other from afar ever since he put in upstream from me. Slow moving and deliberate, he had taken a good long time gearing up, perhaps admiring the slate walls and granite spires that still gave us some morning shade. Pine-scented breezes presaged the summer heat to come.

Although there were no rises to the dries or otherwise, the bite was definitely on before he had even parked his pickup alongside the bank—my first indication that he was not a local, since there was a perfectly good pullout on the other side of the road, just upstream and around the bend a bit. During the last hour and a half alone, I had landed several rainbows in all the shapes, sizes, reticulations, and color tones that the species has to offer. Only two hand-sized browns joined in the three-hooked buffet I was offering of a #18 lint bug, a #20 copper-wrapped black midge, and #14 blue demon. I dappled my nymph train into a few more tea-colored pockets of water up towards my new neighbor and then happily pulled out to go have a snack in my van—certain that he had witnessed my success and would persevere even though he seemed to be spending more time switching flies than actually wetting his line. I've known more than a few fly fishers that like to find a sweet spot and spend the better part of a day sticking it out until they unlock the puzzle, and this guy seemed to be one from that ilk.

Leaving him to his fun in the sun, I rounded the road bend upstream to my home away from home, parked in the last of the remaining shade of late morning. Wafts of solar-heated ponderosas provided incense for my roadside camp as I assembled my two-burner Coleman upon a boulder a few steps away from the steeply angled granite behind. The seemingly endless flow of Estes Park–bound drivers and riders streamed by like migratory salmon in search of recreation and merchandise as I sat sipping my mug of warm dhal, watching the motoring gapers watch me watching them. The Indian spices of my soup and reheated chai seemed particularly invigorating, even though there is no logic for the same food tasting better outdoors than it does in the kitchen. Just as I was considering what section of river to try next, I spotted my New Mexican fishing neighbor coming around the bend. Smiling and making eye contact like he knew me, he geared back down to make a U-turn into my capacious parking area.

My proclivity for a constant cannabis buzz generally inclines me to be a bit stand-offish, so I was clumsily stashing my half-smoked post-lunch bowl of ganja as Mr. New Mexico strode towards me.

Sure smells interestin' over here, he says, inflaming my THC paranoia.

When I saw that he was referring to my leftovers, I relaxed and offered him a cup. He politely declined, preferring to stick to his beef jerky.

I seen ya havin' fun down below earlier, so when I came around the corner I just had to stop and tell somebody who might care.

Care about what? My sativa-enhanced mind braced for a pedantic soliloquy on insect hatches or something of the like.

The biggest dang brown I ever pulled in, man! I can't believe this little river has fish like that.

Oh yeah, they're in there. Where do you usually fish that you'd call this a "little river?" I could feel the spark in his voice that can only come from contact with a trophy fish.

The San Juan is my home stream. Not so unusual to land a twenty-plusser down there.

What'd ya take him on?

She took the sow bug, just this side of that big old boulder you saw me by. Ran me across once but I got her back over somehow.

Nice work! Any ariels?

Naa, but there sure was quite a splash-fest at the netting. Not exactly SOP but it worked out.

Wow, I haven't heard that one in awhile.

You think I'm *lyin'*, man? He laughed.

No, no; I mean "SOP." I haven't heard anyone use that since my uncle. I think he picked it up in the Air Force, among some other *choice* terms.

Yeah, I guess that did come from the Army. You ever serve?

No, but I thank you for yours. My uncle was in Vietnam in the early '70s. He'd send cassettes to my mom instead of letters mostly; you could hear shelling or bombs or whatever in the background sometimes. This seemed to change his tone.

I got to spend some *quality* time over there myself. In fact, it was right after I got back in '69 that I got into fly fishing full tilt. I guess being on the water helps me *cast out* my demons, so to speak.

I think I know what you're talking about. I read a book by a Vietnam vet who pretty much did the same thing with bears in Yellowstone.

Bears, fish, beers; we all find our way one way or the other, or we don't.

He had been looking towards the river ever since walking up, but with those last words his eyes turned to the sky and I wondered what lost souls he might be remembering. We commiserated about the lack of current television programs of the pertinence and persistence that *MASH* had had for Vietnam. Our beloved USA was hot into wars in Iraq and Afghanistan at the time, and the paucity of oppositional voices seemed deafening to us both. Sleeping puppies watching over the drunken kittens in charge of the show was pretty much our collective assessment of mass media journalism.

As my new New Mexican acquaintance spun his ride back around towards Estes, I reassessed my *supply* situation and opted to pack it up and head to Greeley for more herbs rather than do any more fishing during what was becoming a very warm afternoon.

Living so close to the mouth of the Big Thompson in Loveland is ideal for someone who likes to fish every other day or so but the print shop where I work, and my fellow pressman and marijuana supplier, reside in Greeley. Gerald has always seemed more than a little off-the-grid. I can see the wisdom in consulting a river guide to land a big one or a shaman if in search of psycho/spiritual transformation but, if the latest available strain of indica or sativa is the goal, or maybe an obscure Weld County factoid, Gerald is a great resource. He graduated in '69 from Greeley Central High School and has since become the Hunter S. Thompson of Agua Caliente (his nickname for Paradise Acres mobile home park).

Watching his 6'2" scarecrow frame with a peg cane shuffling towards my van, I crack a thankful smile that he is still alive at all. Canadian whiskey and oxycodone capsules nearly did him in a few years ago, with the happy result of a new lease on life free of both. After all, can anyone *really* live who has never seen a need for salvation? Sure the self-righteous rich and un-self-examined have most of the stuff and power, but it is the poor who have spirit and lives. Many would love to trade their responsibilities for a fishing rod and a quiet place to use it; my motto "Fish First!" has always served me well and I imagine the consequences will catch up with me someday . . . hopefully after I am long expired.

What are you thinkin' today? Disc golf? Roma's Pizza? J.B.'s? Where we goin'?

He knows my Greeley predilections well, yet he forgot to mention the most important one.

I was hoping on findin' some herbs, *if* you happen to know of any available?

I can do better than *know*. I went ahead and picked you up an eighth of primo at Bert's last night.

You're the man, dude. Thanks! I guess that increases our options exponentially. What do you wanna do?

He unscrewed the top of his cane and slipped out a tightly wrapped baggie of pungent green and red nuggets.

Smoking some of this Durban Poison would be pretty high on my list.

Let's do it up! I got my fishin' stuff still on board. Didn't you say once that there's somewhere in La Salle where you can mess around on the Platte?

If Woody Creek is Hunter S. Thompson's home water, the South Platte drainage below Denver, Commerce City, and all the way to the inflow of the Poudre River is Gerald's place. His surname is well-respected locally due to an uncle and brother who are high-ranking municipal employees in Greeley, as well as for another paternal uncle who was amongst the 191st Tank Battalion, which initially liberated the Dachau concentration camp. When I asked him once what his apparently conservative family thought about him burning his draft card and riding a bus with "Hanoi Jane" back in the '70s, he nonchalantly replied that his dad and uncles eventually saw the mess it was, and his brother, who did a tour in '67–'68, outright told him not to go. Gerald was formally pardoned in '76 by the president sharing his name, even though he had consorted with The Weathermen.

Sure is getting hot for May; you sure you wanna fish?

I'll just wade in some old sneakers and a swim suit. It'll be a great way to cool off.

The place he led us to turned out to be a State Wildlife Area that had been closed after a flood a couple of years back. The overgrown lot was gated off, but there was some parking available under some cottonwoods, near the massive bridge spanning the South Platte. Only two vehicles were parked on the other side, but the copious trash and other human refuse all along the roadside implied a certain popularity. As we walked to the river proper, we saw a Mexican family upstream, with bicycles and inner tubes for the kids on the wide sand and gravel beach. The graffiti-splashed bridge supports we walked under to head downstream offered some nice shade but Gerald decided to follow me until the sand terminated at a six-foot-high cut bank. What looked to be a beaver dam was really some old scrap iron enmeshed with concrete rip-raff and other random detritus that had accumulated just beyond a mini-oxbow.

The pile of crap I ended up casting towards was well-shaded with willow and weeds. What I assumed to be carp were lazily rising inches from the bank. It took a few drifts to get my #20 Renegade into the soft, foamy flat water where a good-sized sucker vacuumed it in and went nuts. I was fortunate I brought the 6–7 weight rod; this fish did not know the rules about giving it up easily to be released in good order. After Gerald snapped some pictures, I tried to let the poor, slimy thing go into a shallow side stream, but it just sat in one place—pointing to Commerce City.

Little did we know, we had been under surveillance. A heavily tattooed guy in his twenties came out from under the bridge and asked me if he could "grab that fish." I was surprised to see him run off the other way back upstream since I had replied in the affirmative, but he returned with an aluminum landing net and scooped up his prize without a chase. He thanked me with a toothy smile as he trotted back to their picnic. Minutes later, our grateful amigo came back with a handful of homemade tortillas and a perfectly grilled slab of seasoned beef flank. He even produced a couple of cans of Sam's Club grape sodas from his deep pockets before he left us to our unexpected feast. We sat in the sun and sand and lost track of time, laughing and eating heartily as we looked back through the photos we had taken on my digital camera and on his cell phone. When we saw one particular closeup of the "trophy" carp, adorned with lesions and tumors, missing a fin or two, but still looking proud as I held him close to my fly rod, Gerald said, "You know, according to the Viet Cong, everybody who survives is the winner; and the dead from *both* sides are revered equally. I guess we just see it differently over here."

*A true outdoorsman, dubbed "Nature Boy" by his mother, T. M. has been collecting real and imagined tales of the wild for decades. From Nebraska's sandy Platte to Colorado's Big T, rivers have been the ephemeral constant providing guidance and wisdom throughout T. M.'s unconventional yet charmed journey through life.*

# A Hole You Never Fill

## Richard Welch

A sinking ship in a dark sea leaves a wake of horror and emptiness. I hold my beloved father's hand and he gives the slightest squeeze good-bye. I assure him that I will be right back. Despite what is diagnosed as a brain aneurism, I know he understands. I explain that I just need to take a quick shower and change the clothes I threw on this morning after he called. When I return, he no longer understands. Soon the irregular beat turns into a flat line and the nurse, head down, quietly turns off the monitor.

How can this happen to a loving, witty, intelligent father of five children; to a cherished college professor on the day of his happily anticipated retirement; to a modest war hero who left college, joined the Army as a private, and survived the bloody Pacific island-hopping; to a sixty-five-year-old man who was just recovering his spirits after two years of grieving the loss of his younger wife? I cannot begin to think of answering the unanswerable. I can only mindlessly plod through funeral details and, then, escape. Nothing is fair; nothing makes sense.

I do not grieve by crying or by reminiscing. I simply take a plane from Boston to Idaho. I leave. I flee. I escape. I try to keep my mind blank, but I cannot forget that slight squeeze of good-bye.

I made my way to a small cabin in Pierre's Hole, Idaho. Some time ago, the local Chamber of Commerce renamed the area Teton Valley in a still unsuccessful effort to attract dudes and other vacationers from the chic eastern side of the Tetons, namely, the much envied Jackson Hole, Wyoming. Luckily, the Chamber of Commerce failed, and one can still find in this hole the wild, romantic beauty about which historian Bernard DeVoto rhapsodized. Lush barley and potato fields border the peaceful spring creek that bisects the valley. To the west lie the Big Hole Mountains and, to the east, the spectacular Tetons loom above the foothills. It is no wonder that Jedediah Smith, the Sublettes, and the rest of the early mountain men decided to hold their most famous summer rendezvous on this side of the Tetons.

But, the last thing I wanted was quiet reflection in the shadow of the Teton peaks. I needed to keep moving; the massive stands of cedar, spruce, and fir of northern Idaho beckoned. Mary Kate, my longtime if fading girlfriend, called, probably to check on my mental state. She listened with quiet concern when I told her that I was leaving immediately for a long roadtrip. After a few difficult moments she wished me a safe voyage. Always one with a streak of religion, she added, "I'll pray for you, and I've asked God to kiss you on the forehead."

If only I possessed this Catholic girl's comforting belief. She knew that I am cut from a more agnostic cloth and she simply sighed when I tried to present a brave, frivolous front by responding that I hoped that I would not need too much divine guidance to capture eager west slope cutthroat trout. With her benediction, I loaded my rental car and headed for the panhandle.

My drive began in the dreary lava beds of southern Idaho, my mood matching the dark craggy vista. I was glad to escape the dark sage-pocked rock slabs and reach the grim town of Mud Lake, Idaho. Slowing to thirty miles per hour, I looked at a streetfront fit for Edward Hooper: a farm implement showroom, an abandoned grocery store, and a bar. Mud Lake: the name said it all. This was followed by boring miles of sage brush, "no trespassing" signs, and barbed-wired nuclear reactors . Welcome to the federal government's National Engineering Laboratory. The blue highway sign chirps, "Quality People Doing Quality Research." Thoughts of hazardous nuclear waste and government minions pressed my foot to the gas pedal.

The scenery improved as I coasted through the lonely Lemhi Valley. I felt lucky to find a gas station that sold candy bars on this two-hundred-mile stretch. Children who grew up in the now nearly abandoned towns of Lone Pine, Hahn, and Gilmore must have been overjoyed to leave these windy, barren hills behind. I felt the heavy weight of depression and scanned the dial for an upbeat song. No radio station reached the depths of the Lemhi.

Dropping into the lush Bitterroot Valley of Montana was a startling contrast to the quiet, Mormon-dominated confines of eastern Idaho. The bars proudly advertised two-for-one drinks, dancing, poker, and who knows what else. It sounded rather tempting, but it was only early afternoon.

Because no roads travel north through the incredibly rugged mountains of northern Idaho, one must detour through Montana to reach the Idaho panhandle. My goal was the neat, modest town of Superior, Montana. Superior, labeled a city by Montana standards, seemed frozen in the Eisenhower administration. Mary Kate and I had discovered an excellent café here while repairing a tire during an earlier camping trip. Fortunately, from my point of view, she had run out of clean bras and was bouncing about in a t-shirt as we entered the café. This sight raised a few Stetsons and ball caps at the counter, and Mary

Kate, pink blotches spreading on her cheeks, whispered, "they all must think I'm some Mountain Mama, let's sit down quickly." Smiling at the memory, I ate the still superb homemade pie washed down by the regionally weak coffee.

There is a pleasure in turning off a highway and onto a gravel road. My atlas assured me that this was the forest road that led to Hoodoo Pass and back into the wilds of Idaho. Why anyone termed Hoodoo Pass a mountain pass remains a mystery. It is a winding gravel road running over the tallest mountain in the vicinity. Perhaps showing the laissez-faire philosophy popular in these parts, guardrails do not exist. The logging trucks that barrel down these roads raise enough dust to blind any driver within a half mile of the lumbering beasts. There is a reason why old Jim Bridger never bothered with this pass and why Meriwether Lewis was guided another way.

The four cylinders strained over the pass. The downhill slope was steep, with views of unbroken forest and mountains. The sound of crunching gravel was covered by the noise of exploding tires. On the steep downgrade, steering was nearly impossible. Of course, there was no place to pull over to figure out the problem. As I wrestled the wheel, knowing I had but one spare, I hoped that only a single tire blew out.

I finally reached level ground, stopped, and discovered that God had at least kissed the car on the forehead. I had panicked. The tires were fine. This tenderfoot wasn't used to washboard gravel of a real man's road. Maybe I should have stopped for those two-for-one drinks.

At ten o'clock the nearly endless daylight of a northern Idaho summer was beginning to wane as I pulled into the Kelly Creek campground. The campground, hardly a slice of wilderness beauty, was a series of randomly placed fire rings, a few trucks and horse trailers strewn about a meadow, and a fair amount of horse manure. It all looked fine to my travel-weary bones, and I happily pitched a tent and started a fire. A mule deer roamed the overlooking hill, stopped, and stared at me.

After replacing the ever fractured mantles on my Coleman lantern, I hustled into my well-worn sleeping bag with an aluminum cup of sixteen-year-old Scotch and a hook-and-bullet article about this very creek. Kelly Creek is nearly famous; it has been touted by the fly fishing heavyweights—people who fish throughout the world and actually make some sort of living by writing about fish, flies, and tackle. I find such kiss-and-tell pieces unsettling and vaguely immoral, and I read them avidly. This magazine article stuck to the formula and described the deep-bodied cutthroats striking various attractor patterns with abandon. I read by the light of the wheezing old Coleman about how the air sparked, the water rushed clean and clear, and how one escaped the twentieth century by fly fishing on this wilderness stream. Perhaps not Traver or Mclean, but it was enough to get the adrenaline running in this armchair angler. I dozed off on my always brutally hard foam mattress, exhausted.

Someone cranked up a generator. The sky was still gray; the sun wouldn't shine into the canyon for hours. I lolled about in my sleeping bag not wanting to face the cold dew and wondered how heavy my pack was going to feel.

The hike to my camping spot was only about four miles, but I never had prided myself on being a pack horse.

I crouched down and hoisted the pack on my back. It felt punishingly heavy, much heavier than the last time I made this trip. And, of course, it was. The last time I hiked this stretch was with Mary Kate. A generous and strong woman, she cheerfully split the load. I felt no aching loneliness without her, but I now missed her good humor and strong back. As I trudged toward the trail, a blacktail doe near the trailhead stopped her grazing to look up at this sorry sight; she seemed unburdened.

I started at a fast clip but soon my pace dropped off, until I was simply putting one foot in front of the other. My mind began to wander. I likened myself to Nick Adams hiking off to find solitude and solace along a trout stream after confronting the shattering experience of death. The thought helped for about the first two miles. Thereafter, I focused on the spectacular scenery of browse-covered hills, old burned-out snags, the shallow riffles and the deeper green pools. This was the land of the Big Burn of 1910 when hurricane-force winds concentrated numerous wildfires into a fireball that burned an area the size of Connecticut. The blackened snags still stand like sentinels over and among the spruce and underbrush. The miles passed slowly. I rounded a corner and spied my destination. You could not miss it, a beautiful grove of fir and ferns where Cayuse Creek met with the Kelly. I bounced down the hillside from the high trail and confronted four llamas resting placidly among the waist-high ferns. This was a surprise. Closer inspection revealed a bevy of people pitching three tents on the far side of the grove. Luckily, the grove was large and the llamas remarkably quiet. I slunk over to an unoccupied clearing hard by the creek.

There is solace in setting up a camp. I snapped the tent poles together, stretched the nylon fly and staked it down, and rolled out the sleeping bag. *No matter what happens now, I have a safe harbor.*

Next I turned to my fishing gear, and fit the smooth, lustrous rod pieces together. With the simple black reel screwed into the silver holder at the rod's base and the heavy peach-colored fly line strung through the guides, I proceeded to tie on the light monofilament leader and, without much thought, selected a fly and tied it onto the leader's end. The rigged rod was beautiful. I leaned back against a large cedar, closed my eyes, and listened to the creek.

Heading upstream, unburdened by my pack, I felt light, almost free. Above Cayuse, long stretches of Kelly Creek are too shallow to hold good-sized fish. I wanted to concentrate on the deeper pockets and pools where the creek enters a deep, boulder-filled canyon. In the past, I enjoyed great success in these pools drifting hopper patterns, getting strike after strike. After a mile, I reached the first promising spot. I deftly angled down from the path and onto the bank. On my first cast my hopper pattern, a slim combination of deer hair and pheasant feathers tied by my friend Jack, drifted downstream untouched. This was puzzling. It was prime hopper time, eleven in the morning. There was a nice breeze and plenty of hoppers danced about the bank vegetation. But Jack always told me, cast and keep moving. And so I went around the bend to the next pool.

There, to my further surprise, was someone whipping a fly line around. This was not the solitude I had expected. I joined the hoppers and clambered up the bank so as not to disturb my competition. No problem, I consoled myself, I will simply hike up a few bends and outdistance this fellow. Still, I could not remember Nick Adams being disturbed by anyone as he fished in Michigan's Upper Peninsula.

As I hiked by, I glanced over at my competition and gave a most insincere smile and wave. Who was this bird? Adorned with a floppy white canvas hat, he was casting enthusiastically, if not expertly, while still wearing his hiking boots and fully loaded backpack. He was a cheerful, even exuberant fellow. "Only small ones so far, how about you?" The accent seemed to beckon more from Appalachia than Idaho. With the floppy hat and an aged pack that sprouted cups, a flashlight, and some tattered clothing, he resembled a vagrant hillbilly.

Before I had a chance to respond, he happily continued: "What'cha using? Every time I fish I try 'em all, but I think I'd do just as good if I stuck with the Renegade." Since using the simple Renegade fly pattern is nearly a religious requirement within the laboring class of Idaho—it is frequently derided by high-priced fishing guides as a "farmer fly"—I decided that perhaps this fellow does hail from the Gem State.

I attempted to avoid answering his first question by answering the second. "I've been using a hopper pattern."

Although I did not consider my comment particularly witty, this guy laughed heartily. "I was using the same damn thing right below here and didn't catch nothing."

I wished him good luck and quickly hiked another half mile up the trail.

A riffle emptied into a modestly deep pool and the current gently swept by a large boulder on the far bank—the stuff of Boston daydreams. This was a perfect cutthroat pool, deep enough to hold good fish, but not so deep as to make them disinterested in feeding on the surface. Those chubby trout could wait in the steady current for the food bouncing down the shallow riffle. Even better, a few smaller fish were dimpling the pool. Confidence regained, I cast through the foot of the pool. Still, no interest in the hopper.

I searched the water's surface fruitlessly for a sign of any insect life. Not a hint of a floating or hatching insect. I concluded, once again, that this "match the hatch" technique, so popular among the famed fly fishers, was highly overrated. Out of deference to Idaho, I clipped off the hopper and rummaged about for a fly named the "sterling trude." It is a peculiar fly created down on the Henry's Fork in southeastern Idaho with a white wing and a bright red bottom. With its colorful rump and peculiar looks, this fly reminded me of a baboon.

Proving the odd nature of fishing, my first cast caught a ten-inch cutthroat. "Like I told you, they all seem small up here!" I quickly turned. There he was again, on the bank, smiling broadly, crooked bottom teeth, pack fully loaded, and hiking boots dripping. How did this bird travel so fast? "Looks like a good pool you got there."

"I hope so," I replied, as cheerfully as possible.

I cast toward the middle of the pool. A beautiful long, fat westslope cutthroat slowly rolled over the trude and put up a dogged fight, running well downstream and stripping line from the reel. This was a hefty fish for such a creek. My companion and I agreed upon the beauty of the fish. He was certainly in a good position to judge because he was now leaning over my shoulder as I removed the fly from the fish.

"Let me see what'cha using." After examining the trude, he hopped up onto the bank and was off again.

The pool brought a few more trout and I felt satisfied as I waded around the bend.

I rather expected to find him at the next pool, so I waved, this time a bit more sincerely, and headed along the trail into the canyon. Three hundred yards later I decided to drop down into the last of the easily accessible canyon pools. It was a beauty:

massive boulders and green swirling water. "Hello there," a voice called from under my foot.

"My god," I mumbled as I jumped back. I had nearly stepped on this guy as he sat eating a peanut butter sandwich in the dark shade of one of the huge boulders. How did this guy travel so fast with that pack? He reminded me of Marley's ghost who, though fettered by chains and cashboxes, traveled endlessly on the wings of the wind. I briefly debated whether I should mention this allusion to Dickens, but he spoke first.

"Go ahead and fish this spot. I'm eating lunch."

I inartfully lied, "Oh no, I just wanted to look it over. I'm going back for lunch now anyway." What moron, I wondered, would believe such a line? "Where," I asked, "are you going to camp?" I wanted to pin down this distraction.

"Well, I just don't know, up along a ways, I suppose." He smiled before taking another bite of the sandwich.

As I walked back to camp, I still felt fully rooted in the late twentieth century. Nick Adams, I thought, where are you?

The grandfather of the neighboring family clan was standing beside my tent on his way to feed the llamas. We conversed about such inanities as a llama's diet, its habits, and its ability to pack heavy loads. Perhaps Grandpa was as bored with the conversation as I was because he suddenly stopped and asked, "So you're camping out here all by yourself?"

"That's right," I replied, probably with a bit of pride and irritation seeping into my voice.

He looked around at my one-man tent, the small camp stove, and solitary pack and shook his head slightly. Without a word he moved off toward his llamas.

The afternoon was hot. I stretched out and slept under the magnificent cedar that shaded my camp. I awoke as late afternoon thunder rolled through the valley.

The hobbled llamas had hopped closer to my tent. At this closer range, they looked rather sweet and dumb. They reminded me of a kindhearted, if somewhat slow, girl I knew in the fourth grade. I stood and slowly approached both the llamas and my tent. Although I was still a full five feet away from the seemingly sweet, dimwitted animals, the closest llama twisted its neck quickly, curled back its lips in a grotesque manner, and vomited foul-smelling greenish-yellow snot on my left shoulder and arm.

As I sat in a small pool, scrubbing my arm and neck with river sand while wringing out my shirt, I looked up at the dark cumulous clouds that had filled the sky and listened to the busy water of the creek. Facing the wilderness and with the stream shielding any sound, I began to weep. The llama's snot was the final straw; how could the world be so unfair, so unfeeling? Objectively, of course, there was no rational basis for this drama. Here I was, a man well into his thirties, a successful hard-nosed federal prosecutor, with enough money to fly out to the wilds of Idaho and fly fish, enjoying good health, whose father had lived a full life. Of course, I cried all the more. Hemingway would have been most disappointed in this emotional wimp. Finally, I lay face first in the stream and dunked my head toward the stony bottom, then stood up, pushed the hair out of my face, and headed to shore.

I grabbed some beef jerky and laid a small fire for the late evening. As I crumpled paper and broke kindling, I noticed that the fire ring was filled with well burnt cans. All part, I reflected, of camping in the late twentieth century.

I fished into the long twilight of a northern Idaho summer evening. Wading in shorts and sneakers from one run to the next, I made short casts and watched my caddis imitation drift like a miniature sail down the golden, glassy runs. By 9:30 I worked my way back to camp. The driftwood was dry and the fire crackled in the darkness. I sipped warm whiskey from my metal cup and thought of the Highland Scots who enjoyed the same endless summer days and frowned on anyone who dared dilute the malt with ice cubes.

I was out of my tent before the sun kissed the canyon walls, planning to hike upstream to the Hanson Meadows. If I waited until the sun was up, the six-mile hike would turn brutally hot. Water bottle and wading shoes strapped to my belt and wearing a fishing vest, I walked quickly to warm myself on this frosty morning. The cold numbed by hands. I opened and closed both the left and right, making fists and switching the rod case from one hand to the other. After two miles, all the cold had left me.

Throughout I kept a close eye out for that bird with the white floppy hat and the backpack. Where did he camp? What if he was already at the meadows dredging every pool? I searched every clearing for sign of his camp and, pleasantly, found nothing.

Halfway through the hike, I skirted a bog and startled a cow moose and a blacktail doe. The moose lumbered off with a hurried, awkward trot, but the doe moved only a few steps, turned back, and watched me climb another ridge. Around the next corner a mule deer buck looked up from the trail and effortlessly hopped off in a series

of high, arching leaps through the deadfall. By this point, I was beginning to believe that the deer had kissed me on the forehead and were watching over me.

At the cliff overlooking the meadows, I regretted my lack of a camera. The creek wound through the boggy meadows like a crystal thread, and the backdrop was uninterrupted, endless fir and pine. There was no sign of another living soul. I thanked God that I was alive and lucky enough to see such places.

My earlier fears proved groundless. The floppy white hat was not in the meadow. Only the Clark's nutcrackers flew noisily from tree to tree. Along a deep run next to the bank, I hauled out four good-sized cutthroats.

The creek turned sharply at the end of the meadow into a forest thick with deadfall and overhanging firs that nearly touched the water. Hoisting over a large dead Douglas fir, I worked my way into the tangled darkness. Ahead of me, still shadowed by tall firs, was the loveliest pool I had ever seen on the Kelly. Several small riffles hit the side of a cliff, joined, and then dumped into a long emerald pool. Trout were rising near the head of the pool. Far from some tangled, tragic swamp, this was paradise.

Having carefully crossed the creek to a small sandy beach below the towering firs, I roll-cast a small parachute Adams into the tail of the pool. The shade was so deep that I could only guess the fly's location. A trout smacked the fly with such a flourish that even a blind man would know to set the hook. A fat westslope cutthroat bulled around the pool, making run after run. More finely spotted trout with green backs, brilliant orange slashes, and full bellies splashed with red spawning colors came to the small fly. I worked the pool for many fish, releasing each back into the liquid emerald. As I reached the riffles that formed the head of the pool, I shouted my joy.

Afterwards, I sat in the meadow, watching two redtailed hawks circle in the endless blue Idaho sky, and prepared my legs for the hike back. I savored the feeling of the sun on my face and the memory of the trout. The llamas, with their green snot and curled lips, seemed far away. The trail climbed steeply out of the meadow. Head down, I put my legs into the task.

I quickly looked up when I heard branches breaking. I first saw the floppy white hat, then the stuffed backpack, and then the wide smile. "Looked like you were having fun at that pool," he shouted as he hopped onto the trail. "I was up on the hillside glassing for elk, and I saw you down in the meadow."

I caught my breath. "Yeah, the fishing was good."

"I thought it would be," he happily responded. "I camped up here in the meadow but left that last pool for you. I was thinking you'd come on up."

I was slightly stunned by his childlike and unfiltered enthusiasm, and the true kindness. I looked closely at his weathered face for the first time. Despite the whiskers, the dirt, and the large reddish nose, there was softness to the face and his clear green eyes sparkled like cool, clear pools.

"Well, I got to get back up that ridge." He quickly turned and headed back through the thick brush and up the steep slope.

"Thank you," I called. Without turning, he raised his right hand in acknowledgment and was quickly swallowed by the small pines and bushes. He moved almost as smoothly and quickly as the mule deer.

A mile from camp, I decided to fish the pool at the end of the canyon. This time there was no one lunching in the shadows of the boulders. I scrambled down and cast from behind a huge rock. A trout slowly drifted up and sucked down the fly. It was the largest of the trip. I placed the spawning male against my rod and saw that he was close to twenty inches. I looked around, hoping in some way that the white floppy hat had materialized so that I could share this incredible fish with him. But, it was only me, and the water, and the rocks. I slid the fish into the pool.

The llamas were gone when I returned to camp. The family had left. I was alone at the junction of two wilderness streams.

The next morning I plucked at least a dozen burnt cans from the fire ring and shoved them into my old pack. It was the least I could do in return.

I expected the hike out to seem shorter than the hike in, but it did not. Repeatedly I assured myself that the trailhead was around the next bend, but then realized that it was still a long distance off as I rounded that bend and gazed ahead. I stretched my back and then scanned the scenery and the changing shadows on the hillsides. Heading up a final incline, I saw the inevitable, a mule deer nodding at me and starting off in the direction of the road as if guiding me back.

*A former federal prosecutor and now a justice of the Massachusetts Superior Court, Richard Welch has been employed as everything from a rivet packer to a freelance journalist, law school professor, and a part-time fishing guide. The author of numerous professional articles, this is his first foray into creative nonfiction. He is currently working on a collection of short stories. He lives with his wife and two sons in Newburyport, Massachusetts and Tetonia, Idaho.*

# Family Currents, Home Waters

## Dean K Miller

The rod arched downward, shaking violently with the strain of a fish struggling to free itself. I grabbed the rod with a quick jerk skyward, setting the hook.

"There's one!" I called out. It had been a long time since I had hooked a fish this strong. The excitement took the edge off the cold, cloudy July morning.

"I'm never on the lucky side of the boat," lamented Danny, my oldest brother.

The fish darted straight downriver. In seconds most of the line zipped off the reel.

"Hey, Dad, it's already down by that other boat," I said, nodding my head toward the aluminum jet-sled sixty yards downstream.

"No, it can't be," he replied.

The steelhead surged out of the water, its large splash nearly wetting their bow.

"Okay, I guess you're right. Let's get her." Dad turned the boat to head downstream.

Keeping constant tension on the fish, I pumped the rod up and down like an oil rig, getting a bit more line back with each cycle. I saw a silver flash in the water as the fish took off on a second run downstream. Line screamed off the reel and seared the top layer of skin off my thumb as I pressured the spool.

"Keep the tip up," Dad instructed, even though this wasn't my first steelhead.

I smiled. How many times had I heard those same words when my brothers and I fished with him? Dutifully, I raised the rod tip, unsure if he noticed.

As the fish neared, it made one last dart under the

back of the boat and out the other side.

"Watch out for the motor, Deano."

I dipped the rod tip into the water, guiding the line under and away from the motor.

"I've got it clear." My arms tightened from the strain of the fight.

Dad stood ready with the net. With a quick jab, he scooped the gyrating torpedo out of the water and set it on the floorboard.

"Fish in the boat!" I called out. High fives ensued all around.

Hooked on the scale, the steelhead trout weighed just over eleven pounds. It was a beautiful specimen: silver sides with contrasting dark gray hues and spots running the length of her back. The fish's adipose fin was clipped off, indicating it was a hatchery fish, so we could keep her. Thoughts of fresh steelhead on the grill ran through my mind. My brother broke my trance.

"I told you. I'm never on the good side of the boat."

"Hey, I offered you that spot."

"Yeah, sure, whatever," he said. "Nice fish though. Congrats."

The filtering gray clouds relented to the late morning sun as we headed back to the dock. Just as when we were kids, Dad cleaned and filleted the catch while Danny and I unloaded the boat, carrying rods, tackle, and remnants of our morning snacks back to the car. The fillets were packed, ready to freeze for my return to Colorado.

We finished up with lunch at a local burger shack and then headed back to Portland. During the drive I planned the next phase of my return home: a trip to the streams of Mt. Hood.

In those snowmelt tributaries, I spent countless hours of my youth fishing with my brothers. Wading in the cold mountain water, I learned how to "read a river" and how to cast light tackle with a technique similar to fly fishing. I also developed my love for smaller rivers and streams while stalking the wild trout living in their icy realms.

The following day I drove to Still Creek and into my past. Happiness in those days meant a spinning rod and reel, a package of six pretied Eagle Claw hooks, a jar of Patzke salmon eggs, enough gas in the tank, and a few dollars for Dairy Queen afterwards. Everything else was a distraction.

I turned onto a single-lane road enveloped by evergreens taller than I remembered. Random shafts of sunlight penetrated the forest, creating a kaleidoscope of shadow and light. After a few minutes driving I noticed something and recoiled in my seat.

Several new cabins and small homes tucked amongst the trees imposed their presence and suffocated the freedom that once ruled here. I drove on until I reached a construction road block. Disappointed, I started the slow drive back to the highway. However, I wasn't going to leave without spending time with the creek. I stopped and found a trail leading down to the water.

After a short downhill walk I arrived on the bank of Still Creek. I stood and soaked in the sounds. The stream tumbled under a log jam of six fallen trees—its song in sync with the wind murmuring through the limbs of pine trees. The creek flowed against a rock wall and then turned downstream. I leapt onto a large rock overlooking a deep pool, sat down, and inhaled deeply, the cool air settling in my lungs. I was home.

This river was an integral part of my teenage years. My heart stirred as I recalled fishing with my two brothers just upstream from where I sat. Closing my eyes, I drifted with the sound of the water to a distant memory.

"Danny! Danny, come here, quick. I've got one!" I called across the stream.

"Hang on, bro. Hang on. I've got the net."

I played the wiggling trout on my five-foot spinning rod, the river's current providing more resistance than the fish. Danny scooped up the rainbow and lifted it up for me to see.

Just then middle brother Dave walked around the bend, his rubber hip boots strapped through the belt loops of cutoff jeans.

"You're wasting your time with that little thing. You should've been with me." He carried a fish much larger than mine, his finger holding the large trout through its gills.

"No way, man," I said. "Where'd you get that one?" My bravado was deflated.

"Pulled him out of that riffle you walked past five minutes ago. Can't believe you didn't fish it. But thanks for leaving it open."

We all laughed as I held my fish in front of Dave's much bigger catch.

"Your fish is just a hearty meal for mine," he said.

The laughter faded, swallowed by the sound of the churning stream.

Opening my eyes, I stared into the pool below. The patchwork of stones looked close enough to touch, their red, brown and beige colors distinct in the clear water. Against this montage I caught a glimpse of movement. First one, then another and finally a third fingerling trout swam underneath me. Their tails fluttered in the gentle current. They stared back at me, big eyes dominating their heads. The three of them together, like me and my two brothers. My heart settled into a comfortable rhythm as I recalled a different fishing trip with my brothers to Still Creek.

Danny maneuvered the car down a steep incline to within ten feet of the river. In the starless black of the forest, the headlights lit up the bubbling water creating a disco ball effect on the surrounding trees and rocks. We left the car running so as not to drain the battery.

"You got everything you need?" Danny asked as he shut the door.

"Yeah," Dave said without turning around; he was already making his first cast.

"Hey, wait. My jar of eggs is on the backseat," I said, but the car door closed on my words.

"Get'em yourself. I'm fishing," Danny said as he took a position downstream from Dave.

I grabbed the door handle and pulled. Nothing happened. I moved to the front door and pulled the handle. That door wouldn't budge either.

"Hey guys, I think we've got a problem," I called above the rumble of the stream.

After thirty minutes and lots of shouting at each other, we fashioned a latch-hook from a stout limb, opened the door, and retrieved the keys. The excitement of our night adventure punctured, we fished just a few minutes longer. Dave, as usual, caught the only fish.

The memory floated away on the current below. I left Still Creek and my memories, and drove back to Portland.

I hoped to return to the mountain streams of my youth once more before I flew back to Colorado.

At midafternoon the following day I pulled into my dad's driveway. A lifelong fisherman, he's never cast a fly, but I knew he wouldn't pass up a chance to join me on the river. While I stocked a small cooler with food and drink, he grabbed a pair of old tennis shoes so I could wet-wade without ruining the only pair of shoes I'd brought from Colorado. Driving out to the highway, we passed the site of his childhood home, long since torn down, making way for a car dealership.

"One time, back in '47, your grandfather took me fishing. I must've been about eleven or so. We drove up by Bonneville Dam to a place called Tanner Creek Pool. I took you and your brothers there once or twice. I don't know if you remember or not."

I couldn't recall, but didn't interrupt his tale.

"Your Grandpa and I fished with bright red spinners set above red feathered, 4/0 treble hooks. Those hooks, with the feathers on them, were as big as my hand. I couldn't believe we'd catch fish on something like that. We landed five big Chinooks and saw more than fifty others caught. At least that many shook loose before reaching a net. All day long huge fish jumped out of the water and I heard an endless cry of 'fish on.' At the end of the day, my dad let me carry one of the biggest ones to the car. I could barely keep its tail from dragging on the ground. Your grandpa waited for me and laughed that quiet, gentle laugh of his."

As I drove on I glanced at my father and saw a contented smile, one I hadn't seen in a long time. He continued.

"The sad part is, I kept those feathered spinners over forty years, and then they were stolen in 1990. Most of the other gear taken I could replace, but you just can't find those feathered rigs anymore."

There were other stories, including their fishing for sturgeon at Onion Rock on the Columbia River.

"Danny, Dave and I used to go there," I said. "One day, I caught two sturgeons. Both were about four feet in length. We were using smelt that were pretty ripe. We heaved those things as far as we could. And remember when you and I went up by Bonneville Dam to fish? On the way home, the boat trailer got a flat, so I sat in the boat alongside the freeway to keep it safe, while you drove back to get the tire fixed."

"Oh, yeah, I don't think we'd be doing that today, would we? I'd probably end up in jail for abandonment," Dad replied.

Our memories flowed as easily as the waters we fished. We reached the park's entrance and Dad paid the five-dollar fee. I drove to the parking lot nearest the best stretch of river, its location easily recalled.

We continued our conversation near the car as I threaded the orange fly line through the guides of my brother's fly rod. For the first time, I realized it was not only old, but also stout—at least a 6-weight. Compared to my favorite 3-weight I used in

Colorado, it felt heavy in my hands and I had to work around the reel setup for a left-handed angler.

Over the next hour and a half, Dad and I shared moments of our lives, some never mentioned before. Though we couldn't see the river from the parking lot, we heard its rush over the rocks, but neither of us was in any hurry for me to start fishing. Being there, together, was good enough. The evening breeze carried our laughter, tears, and memories back to their beginnings. Eventually, we reached a point in our conversation where what needed to be said had been said. It was time to fish.

After a long hug, we started down the winding path. I remembered my childhood days walking with my father. He carried the fishing rods as we walked through the dew-laden pasture to the Wilson River. The past now present we again made our way to the river. Dad fished here on the Salmon River in his younger days; these currents influenced both of our lives. I didn't want to lose this moment.

At the bridge, I saw the river for the first time in more than thirty years. For all that had changed, I found most everything was still the same. We paused mid-span. I stared upriver. Time slipped away. Energized and yet calm, I felt a blending of youthful exuberance and life's wisdom settle within me.

"It's good to be back. Thanks for being here with me."

Dad placed his hand on top of mine, which rested on the railing.

"Yes it is. Welcome back, Son."

We crossed the bridge and Dad sat on the hand carved wood bench that overlooked the river. I managed my way down the bank and walked a short distance downstream. The cold water swirled around my ankles and crept toward my knees as I reached midstream. Wet-wading in the summertime is my favorite way to fish—icy water numbing my legs, the scent of pine trees floating on the breeze, hawks screeching above, and warming by the campfire in the evening. Fishing like this as a kid meant knowing life at its fullest.

I worked a Royal Adams dry fly trailing a small black ant pattern through the riffles and pools. It took a bit to adjust to the heavy rod, but within ten casts I landed my first fish: a small, brown trout hungry for the ant. I held my catch above my head in salute.

Dad flashed a big smile and gave a thumbs-up. The master acknowledged his protégé, a father simply loving his son.

Over the next hour I discovered that maybe I had changed with the passage of time.

In the days long since passed, I would rush from riffle to pothole and then to the next riffle, chasing the currents to find fish. However, on this evening I moved in harmony with the river, fishing at a relaxed pace. Maybe it was because Dad was with me, and I wanted the evening to last longer than it could. Or possibly I wanted to relish my return home, knowing I couldn't stay long. But I knew that a part of me would always remain here.

As I fished my way upstream toward the bridge, Dad came down and joined me. I landed a few more trout as dusk settled in, the fingers of sunlight no longer reaching the river. We walked up the bank and headed back to the car.

"If you want, I can carry the rod," he said, holding out his hand.

I smiled. Nothing had changed. I was still that same kid lucky enough to go fishing with his father. I handed him the fly rod.

"Sure, Dad. Thanks."

*Miller is a freelance writer, professional member of Northern Colorado Writers, and published author through Hot Chocolate Press. He co-founded the Platte Rivers Chapter of Project Healing Waters Fly Fishing, which serves military personnel in Southern Wyoming and Northern Colorado. A native of Portland, Oregon, he fished the streams that drained Mt. Hood in his youth. Employed for twenty-eight years as an air traffic controller with the Federal Aviation Administration, he fishes and writes in Loveland, Colorado.* He is the creator of The Haiku for You Project. Learn more at www.deankmiller.com.

# A Perfect Day

## Kerrie L. Flanagan

Carrie and I jumped back into the car. I turned on the engine, hoping for an instant blast of heat, but it too had to warm up. The temperature gauge read 37 degrees outside; maybe a little cold to be standing in a river, trying to catch fish we were only going to release back into the frigid water.

That morning when I picked Carrie up, I thought it was late enough that it would be warmer outside. Even with the sun shining, the temperature gauge showed otherwise. But we were determined to fish and nothing was going to stop us.

We laughed at our craziness for being here, our breath visible in the air, but excitement filled us at the same time. Carrie wanted to learn how to fly fish, even if that meant going in the middle of November. I think my excitement about my newfound fishing obsession had worn off on her.

A few years ago, if someone had asked me my thoughts on fly fishing I would have said it looked complicated and boring. I always teased my fly fishing friends about their passion with the sport because I didn't understand what the big deal was.

So, it came as a surprise to my fly fishing friends when I agreed to be a parent chaperone on a week-long fly fishing trip with my sixteen-year-old daughter and twenty other students from Polaris Expeditionary Learning School. I told them I wasn't going because of the fishing, but because I would be cooking for the group, which I love doing.

The third morning, after feeding everyone a hearty breakfast, I relaxed on the bank of the river and watched my daughter fish. I admired the ease with which she cast her line into the water, stripped it in as she followed the current, and then did it again. I sat there, under a crystal blue autumn sky, immersed in what she was doing without any awareness that three hours had passed.

Throughout the trip, I was amazed at how the behavior of the usually energetic, hormonal, friend-centered teenagers changed when they got in the river. I watched them not only learn to fish, but learn to be more comfortable in themselves and with the quiet. My perception of fly fishing shifted and I knew I wanted to stay connected to this world, where time faded away and to-do lists disappeared with the current.

A week after my return, I headed to the Big Thompson River with a friend who is an avid angler. Following a crash course in casting, I slipped into the oversized borrowed waders, grabbed my friend's rod, and stepped into the river. As I prepared for my first cast on the water, my hand trembled slightly from nerves and I prayed I would not make a complete fool of myself.

After a quick review from my friend, I concentrated on the cadence of my casting. Each time my fly landed on the water, my insides tightened up in anticipation of a bite. Following a successful cast, my pink indicator bobbed. I yelled to my friend, but my delay in setting the hook allowed the fish to get away.

As we worked our way upstream, all sense of time drifted downstream. I enjoyed the sunshine, the sound of the river, and being away from the two hundred emails waiting in my inbox. I persevered for four hours until I finally hooked and reeled in my first fish; an eight-inch brown trout. Every nerve in my body screamed with excitement and I couldn't stop smiling. After a high five with my friend, I posed for a picture with the fish before releasing it back into the water.

I never imagined I would soon become one of my obsessed fly fishing friends, who constantly checked the weather and river reports. I invested in all the necessary gear and I craved time on the river, rearranging my schedule so I could be on the water as much as possible, even in the winter.

Earlier, on the way up the canyon, a family of bighorn wished Carrie and I well and didn't mind when we stopped to photograph them. Soon we arrived at my favorite

fishing spot on the river. I was grateful there were no other cars in the gravel parking lot.

The cold hit us the moment we stepped out of the warm car. The sun hadn't yet crested the mountain, but we were ready. The parking lot became our classroom. I gave her a rod, and like my friend had done with me just a year earlier, I explained to her the basics of casting. The way the rod tip goes back and forth as if it were touching ten and two on a clock, stopping briefly at each number. The way this gentle back and forth motion sends out a little more fly line each time.

Like everyone learning to cast, the motions and timing were awkward to her at first. The impatience of not letting the line completely roll out on the back cast before bringing the tip of the rod to the front again. Going way past ten and two with the tip. Not keeping the fly line in the air caused some tangling up. But she soon figured out the cadence and had a beautiful cast going. I had read that women were easier to teach to fly fish because of the gentleness and finesse needed for good casting and Carrie proved that point.

With our lesson complete it was time to get in the water. Carrie slipped on the oversized waders I lent her, while I put on my gear. I then rigged her line with two flies and a pink indicator.

The sun still hid behind the mountain as we stepped into the river. We each took in a quick breath adjusting to this new level of cold. I talked to her about the river and where to find the good pockets of water. We found one. Carrie stripped off some line and began her cast. It took her some time to get into rhythm, but she did. Her flies landed nicely on the water and the pink indicator bobbed along as we watched, hoping it would go under. Nothing. After a few casts, the line started icing up, making it more challenging. Our hands and feet had gone numb. It was time to go to the car to warm up.

I rummaged through my fishing gear, glove box, the middle console, and anywhere I thought I could have put it.

"I swear I had a tiny bottle of cinnamon whiskey stashed somewhere in here." I continued looking. "It would help us warm up."

She laughed at my determination to find something that ended up not being there. I made a mental note to myself to stock my fishing bag with the tiny bottles for such occasions in the future.

We sat and talked, urging the feeling to return to our hands and feet before submerging ourselves back into the flowing ice bath.

Despite there being no whiskey to help, warmth crept back in our limbs and we got out of the car. Sunlight finally peeked its way over the mountain, lighting up the river and hopefully warming and waking the fish. The sunshine felt good as we resumed fishing.

I helped Carrie with her casting and fly placement. She fell back into her newly found rhythm. The sun must have sparked new life into the river because it wasn't long before Carrie's indicator went under the surface and she set the hook.

"I got one! I got one!"

Having been through this a year ago myself, I knew exactly how she felt and I was thrilled for her. "Great job. Okay, guide it over here to my net and let's see what you got."

I scooped the brown trout into the net. It looked to be about eight inches. I took the hook out and put it back in the water so it could catch its breath.

"Time for a picture." I held the fish in the net next to her.

"It's beautiful." She reached in to grab it, and the fish flopped around trying to escape her grasp. She held tighter and took it out of the net. Her smile radiated from her whole body. I snapped the picture and she gently released the fish back into the water. We watched him regain his composure before swimming away.

With newfound zeal, Carrie wanted to feel that rush again. She cast her line back in the water. Scenes from my first fly fishing experience from a year ago popped in and out of my mind. The excitement I felt when I caught a fish, the connection I felt to the outdoors, and the ease with which I could stay grounded in the present moment. My friend took the time to share his passion of the sport with me, hoping to open me up to a new world. It worked. Now I had the chance to pay it forward and share my love of fishing with my friend.

Because she had the hang of it, I left Carrie on her own and I moved a little upstream to get my line wet. Like the river, our conversation flowed. "See if you can get the flies over by that rock." "How are your kids?" "Nice job on that cast." "Tell me about your recent backpacking trip."

Over the course of the afternoon, I caught a few and Carrie caught one more. The temperature rose to 47 degrees, but the chilly air no longer bothered us. It was all about friendship, fish, and connecting with nature. A perfect day.

*Kerrie Flanagan is an avid fly fisherwoman and an avid writer. She has written and published hundreds of articles in a variety of different publications including* The Drake, Writer's Digest, *and* Family Motor Coaching. *As the Executive Director of Northern Colorado Writers, she supports and encourages other writers. Her passion for fly fishing rose to the surface a few years ago and she enjoys casting a line out whenever she can. She is the author of* Planes, Trains and Chuck & Eddie; Write Away: A Year of Musings and Motivations for Writers; *and* Claire's Christmas Catastrophe.

# The Drive-in Hole

## Milt Mays

Two things a man needs when he crosses into late fall: love and a good hobby. I guess there's three. Warmth. You get that inside with the first two, but outside warmth becomes more important as the first days of winter approach. Guess that's why I've moved my late fall fishing closer to summer. It gives me two out of three.

The oars creak, the September sun warms my shoulder, and I sit in the front seat of the wooden drift boat Scott made, changing my fly for the next hole on the Bighorn. In the first casts on the last hole, my shoulder reminded me of thousands in the past. Time also taught me it's time for a hopper.

My turn for the oars will come, but not now. Scott knows it. He's probably smiling at the back of my head, knowing my craving for the crash of a big brown on a hopper, and knowing my love of this particular hole on this particular river. Scott rows expertly, the sun-flash of the wooden oars slurping in and out of flowing water. He rows so smoothly that movement is imperceptible. We slide into the perfect angle of drift, allowing the powerful river as wide as a football field to take us right where the fish lay. I am lucky Scott is my friend.

Murmurs and laughs from the guys in the boat behind us; a hawk screams and soars above; the cottonwoods lining the shore flutter their leaves like apple-green butterflies; the tea-colored river gurgles and rushes; and I let out a breath, easing the frustrations of life, concentrating on the moment. I finish tying the hopper, clip off extra mono, and stand, pulling out a few more feet of line, flexing the rod, hearing the click-click of an old Hardy reel, squinting into the glare, ready to cast, not needing a rise, only a particular riffle that flows into smooth water.

We float around the bend and there they are: smashed and rusted cars packed like sardines on the outer bend. Clumps of long grass grow out absent windshields, waving in the wind. The cars prevented erosion and created a deep current for the browns, and my memory. Their crushed history oozes out. They've traveled thousands of miles, experienced the lives of children, beautiful women, and haggard old men, smelled the smoke of Marlboros mixed with fish slime and river mud, tasted the dribble of chocolate-dipped ice cream cones while motoring home on a hot Montana night to Billings or Hardin or Fort Smith. Given the location of their final resting place on this bend of the Bighorn River, joyful stories of a bent rod from a large trout must have echoed off their dashboards and soaked into their seat cushions. But fishing tales are only the opening act the cars heard. For it is not just fishing that forges friendship. It is

trust to share stories of lives and families, like the guys in our two boats. There's Carl, wondering how to tame a teenage daughter who wears shorts too tight and has a worthless boyfriend with purple, Mohawk hair. Steve cried once, telling about his Alzheimer's dad not recognizing him last Christmas. Jim paid for a Vegas vacation for his quiet, farming parents who put him through law school. Scott proudly smiled when he told me of his stuttering son's science project winning first place at the science fair, then gritted his teeth after that son returned from Afghanistan in a box. I guess I bored them with stories of my wife and her years of dedication to this grumpy guy who'd returned from a war, cynical and crass. Lora had waited and hoped while I slopped through a green jungle I can't forget. I came back. We carried on. Lora mellowed me out. How I loved her.

I look at the cars. I know I can squeeze happy stories from their seats, turn their radios to the memory channel, and listen to tales better than any guide about honey holes and secret flies. Though the grill of the Chevy or the rear fins of the Buick were crushed by the junk yard, their lines of hood and fender and orientation of taillights reveal a uniqueness, as individual as the men who drove them to explore these waters.

Scott's handmade drift boat floats through this current of old cars. I feel the pull of the line on the rod with each back cast. In the fields above the river, the rusty-hinge call of a pheasant sounds like the opening door of the '57 Chevy I drove down Main Street on a summer night, and I'm there. War and terror dissolve like the morning mist off the water.

The throb of the 283, four barrel, V8 massages my spirit and I hug Lora closer. Her firm breasts press my side and I wave to a friend passing in his Ford Fairlane. I love her, my Chevy, and my country, a country that rivals the Roman Empire, led by a war hero president who promises to end communism. Lora's blond hair tickles my cheek; her soft skin and musky smell nuzzle my neck. I feel her squeeze my leg like it's yesterday, sitting next to me on bench seats, a closeness that sexy bucket seats have killed. Five years later I was drafted.

I cast the hopper below the Chevy's rusted tail fin. The orange and brown of the foam hopper takes me back to the A&W.

I park the Chevy at the drive-in space and order on the pushbutton intercom from a sweet-voiced teenage girl who delivers floats and fries on the tray boy and fits it on the partially rolled-up window. After a hot summer afternoon of two-a-day football practice, nothing quenches a thirst better than an A&W root beer float. There's no place better to sit and talk with Lora, mulling weekend plans while listening to the radio play Buddy Holly's "That'll Be the Day." The first gulp is always too much, the ice-cream headache as fresh as the morning breeze is now on my face.

The hopper floats by the grill of a '52 Ford truck, emphasizing what trucks have lost in distinctiveness that hoppers have maintained. Each fly tier has its own special pattern: one more modern with bright orange foam, sprouting yellow rubber legs; the other one traditional, brown and sleek, using only natural feather and fur.

My orange foam hopper floats twenty feet downstream from Scott's slim feather pattern, almost obscured by the morning sun glaring off the calm riffles in the Drive-in Hole. I envy his use of the traditional pattern, but my old eyes need bright colors.

A crashing strike breaks the calm. I lift the rod, feel the headshake and pull of the big trout, laugh and marvel at the struggle on either end of the line, that logic and thought and creativity can occasionally overcome a billion years of evolutionary cautious instinct and timidity of prey. That same human logic created the beautiful and unique lines of the old cars and crushed and stacked them on the bend of this river to prevent erosion, but never foresaw how those old rusted cars could enhance the individuality of a sport that really makes no sense, just as all art. But oh what peace those cars bring to the soul on a cool summer morning when a man whose life is all but spent can make an instant of reality meld with a lifetime of memories; where a slimy, cold-blooded fish and rusted old cars can soothe an old curmudgeon.

We drift by the end of the cars and I finish the fight, and feel the wars, family crises, and personal shortcomings slip away with each run of the brown trout. Bringing *Salmo trutta* to the net, I marvel at the color and strength of a creature with no arms or legs, a wriggling solid muscle as wondrous and unique as the hand with opposable thumbs that grips it. Knowing eyes stare into my being, releasing demons I should never have stored, lancing boils of life without a blink. Once again I realize this sport, this art of fly fishing, has soaked my soul in a time I thought was lost, a beauty I thought humanity had killed. The cars cast out as junk and stacked as an erosion barrier on the bend of a mighty river are instead a new window to an American era of automobile creations that fuse with the uniqueness of each cast, each fly, and the struggle of each fish.

Delivering the red-spotted wonder back into the depths of the Bighorn, the last flip of its tail fades with the upstream vision of rusted cars, and I smile, knowing I must come back again for the glorious salve of fly fishing the Drive-in Hole on the Bighorn River.

*Milt grew up in Colorado, though he spent most of his adult life as a Navy doctor. After graduating from the Naval Academy and medical school, he traveled all over the world with the Navy and Marines, and finally came back to rest in Colorado. He's worked as a fly fishing guide, and currently is a primary care doctor for the VA. Other published works by Milt include novels* The Guide, Dan's War, *and* The Next Day, *and short stories "Thanksgiving with Riley" and "The Dry-Land Farmer." He lives with his wife in Colorado. Milt's website is www.miltmays.com.*

# The Old Yellow Fishing Dog (A Love Story)

## Louis Phillippe

We never know where we will find love, or rather, where love will find us. Sometimes it appears from an unlikely source, but often it comes precisely when needed to help heal wounds inflicted by events beyond our control.

The sad yellow pup waited at the front of the cage to meet my wife, ribs and hip bones protruding ahead of a tentatively wagging tail, a pitifully abused face pleading to be noticed, to be shown kindness for perhaps the first time in her life. In her short eight months she'd been starved and mistreated, beaten so badly that one eye was useless. But her good eye gleamed with a vibrancy that belied her emaciated, greyhound-thin body.

"But I don't want another dog!" I whined when Gail proposed the idea. We already had two, neither truly "mine." I hadn't had my own companion since the rough ending to my previous marriage cratered with the accidental killing of my beloved Chessie by my ex. Two dogs in the house were enough, I figured, even though one old neurotic pound refugee we'd adopted was nearing life's end. I was armpit-deep into a high-stakes career I no longer enjoyed and that was slowly killing me. What kept me sane was fly fishing on the stream that runs below our Colorado mountain cabin. That was my place of rejuvenation. Dealing with another screwed-up dog was the last thing I needed with my weekly travel for a pressure-cooker career. My job was to feed the Wall Street beast, a relentless monster that grew more demanding by the quarter.

So I wasn't pleased when Gail returned with it the next day, put the other two out in the yard, and brought it in to meet me. I didn't need to feign disinterest—it was genuine. Look at this mess of a dog, I thought. Ugliest thing I've ever seen.

"Before you jump to conclusions," Gail began, "she's been sick and had worms. Whoever had her before didn't feed her right, either. But she's really sweet, and I can fatten her up. Will you please give her a chance? She needs us. Otherwise they're going to euth her." My wife, bless her giant heart, sometimes brings home damaged animals that need a home, like the sweet old crippled rabbit with the wrecked back legs we cared for until his death. Some asshole had tried to run him over with a motorcycle to punish his girlfriend. Here we go again with another one, I fumed.

She marched right up to me, sat at my feet, gazed up at me with that one good eye filled with hope, and placed a paw on my thigh. I was hooked. I got up and walked into the kitchen for a beer, and she followed in a natural heel. I returned to my chair, where she sat next to me watching over the room. "This is MY dog!" I called out to my wife.

The next morning Gail insisted I take Maggie fishing. I protested, not wanting to mess with an unruly dog on a technical stream while navigating willows, deadfalls, beaver dams, and very likely moose. "I think she'll be fine," Gail insisted. "Take the leash. If she's a problem, call me and I'll come get her."

We didn't need the leash on the walk down the hill. Maggie took an unusual interest in my every move and paced beside me. When I stopped on the trail below the first pool to see what she'd do, preparing for the worst, she studied *me* to see what *I* had planned. I knelt down and eased forward, flicking a couple quick false casts, now as interested in this dog as in the browns dimpling at the head of the run. She watched the fly land on the water, the take, the short battle, then eased forward and nosed the net as I slipped the hook from the spotted trout's jaw. After allowing a quick lick I released the fish. She stuck her pink nose into the water and bubbled around, searching for it. She was apparently born into the Fishing Dog profession. I stroked and praised her as she lifted up her snout and hit me with a sloppy wet lick across the cheek. Our deep and enduring love affair was cemented in that moment.

This was a dog that needed someone like me: someone who had once had a devoted, intelligent fishing and hunting partner and appreciated the magical bond shared between two like-minded creatures. She needed me after the torture inflicted during her short life to that point. I needed her as a buffer against my Sisyphean curse of pushing a monstrous profit boulder up an ever-steepening slope.

True to her word, Gail quickly fattened her up, and as she filled out she began to

exhibit excellent conformation. She became a gorgeous blonde specimen of Labrador Retriever. Well muscled and sharply cut, people would regularly remark about her stature before asking what happened to her eye. I had no answer for that. But I slowly recognized this: My fishing was becoming less about catching trout and more about adventuring with *her*. My weekly mangling by the Fortune 500 meat-grinder grew more tolerable as I looked forward to returning home to be with my wife, our growing daughter, and this magnificent fishing dog.

The old pound dog passed on not long after. We were left with Maggie and our Australian terrier, which had become Maggie's constant play companion. They rolled and wrestled nonstop, but when it came time to fish, Maggie was full-on business. She knew all the clues, beginning with the placing of my tool lanyard on the basement bench before rigging up. From that moment on until we arrived at the first pool, she was glued to my side, patiently waiting for the first cast to land. She watched the fly as it progressed downstream and tensed in anticipation when the strike occurred. If I nymph fished with a bobber, she was mesmerized by the little float drifting toward us. Before long she began to herd the trout into the net, nosing them gently, staying clear of the delicate tippet, never biting at them like so many other fishing dogs I knew. She wouldn't enter the water unless I did. Then she'd wade beside me until the current became too swift or the water too deep, where she would slip in behind me and paddle slowly in my eddy. If I asked her to stay on the shore, all it took was an open hand facing her and she would sit and watch until invited to join me.

I taught her none of this. She just seemed to *know*. There was no e-collar involved, no pocketful of treats, no repeated lessons at the end of the leash with sharp voice commands. We fished as one cohesive unit, man and dog, a union that amazed me every time we went afield. Soon I was able to leave the boiling ball of enmity behind whenever we were together. Within a few months I began to long for her company when away on weekly business trips. I changed my fishing preferences too, planning more outings on waters where she could come along.

I preside over the large fishery where we live, and as part of my volunteer duties I stock truckloads of fish into the ponds and lakes for property owners to yank out and

plop into a skillet. We all understand the rationale, a compromise that leaves the streams as catch and release wild trout havens for those few who are willing to weave through the willows to reach spooky little wild trout. As is common with fish trucked in from afar, a few don't weather the journey and end up floating out into the lake, carried by the current. One day I threw a rock out toward a floater and commanded her to

fetch. I'd never formally taught this skill, as my bird hunting days were long behind. On queue she plunged into the lake, swam directly to the trout, mouthed it gently, brought it ashore, and delicately dropped it at my feet, looking up expectantly. Of course I tossed another rock, but she was already onto the game. She retrieved every trout, some by hand signals when she was far from shore. None had even a scale disturbed. She seemed immensely pleased and proud that she, too, was able to catch fish. Except this time, instead of releasing them, we kept them (which she surely wished we'd do every time).

We offered them to a crew of Hispanic laborers finishing cement at a nearby cabin, who had been watching the show in amazement. One who spoke fluent English asked how long it had taken me to teach her that. I told him I didn't, that it was her first time. He turned to the crew and explained in Spanish. They knelt down and took turns petting her, mumbling and staring open-mouthed as if she were a dog saint of some sort. She soaked up the adulation, glancing sideways at me to make sure I noticed. Retrieving floaters is now a highlight of our bi-weekly stockings, and she's terribly disappointed if all of our expensive trout manage to survive the trip.

Sometimes I fish on a nearby lake in the evenings, and we like to stand on a large sandstone rock out in the water that's just big enough for the two of us. If someone else is on "our" rock, she will look at me, look at them, and sometimes trot over to deliver an evil-eye signal that they need to move because it's not "their" rock. Friends now know this, and will surrender the rock to her when we arrive. If one of them is catching fish and I'm not, she'll wander over to him and sit for a while, glancing back furtively at me as if to ask, "What's he doing that you're not? C'mon, get with the program or I'm leaving you!"

As the years passed I became more of a challenge for Gail. She was the anchor who held together our daily lives, our home, and a mountain cabin. She drove to the grocery store while I rode limos in London. She managed our household finances while I managed nine-figure deals in Buenos Aires. She fed and watered the dogs in the kitchen, while I fed Chateaubriand to technology executives in New York and watered them with hundred dollar bottles of Opus One. When I came home, cranky from jet-lag, she was patient as I recalibrated. She was always ready with a home-cooked meal, though she'd prefer dinner at a restaurant after a week home alone. This was a weekly ordeal, but her love and patience held fast.

Maggie was always there for me too, greeting me at the door with a bone, forgiving my foul moods, ever ready to hike up the trail into the forest to fish. I had helped heal her after her abuse and death sentence. She was helping to heal me in her own intuitive way. If I sat on the couch to read or watch television she would ask to climb up, curling beside me with her head on my thigh. When in my chair, she became a seventy-pound lap dog. At night she would sneak up onto the bed and gently snuggle beside my feet.

Finally the pressure reached critical mass, taking a physical and emotional toll. Gail is eight years younger, so I knew she'd likely outlive me anyway. But Maggie was aging, and the honest truth is that I wanted to spend as much time with her as possible in the span we had left together. I was drinking more than I should, mostly to quiet the noise and push the beast back into the shadows. This was hard on Gail, too, but it was our livelihood, my career, and I couldn't just walk away and start flipping burgers.

We figured out that if we were careful with our investments, with a little luck, I could trade the Silicon Valley maelstrom for calmer waters. Maggie enthusiastically voted for this decision. We held our breath and took the plunge, and within weeks the snaky tangle of anxiety and tension began to unravel. Maggie and I fished, hiked, and camped constantly that first summer, urged on by my supportive wife who could see the healing taking place. The pace of life began to slow, the sense of urgency dissipating.

Now Maggie and I are both sixty-one. I have a titanium hip and she has a touch of arthritis in one shoulder. Our hearing isn't what it used to be and her one good eye makes up for my two fading ones. But we are both young at heart, relishing every moment together, always ready to hike down a river canyon or over a mountain.

Life carries no guarantees. I once guided a famous bomber pilot, a highly decorated veteran of three wars. He was a real stud of a man, in excellent shape. That morning, fresh snow reflected off the low clouds just after sunrise, creating a surreal purple and gold aura around us. He told me it was the most beautiful morning he'd ever seen. Ten minutes later I was desperately trying to pump life back into him. I failed. One moment he was basking in nature's gift. The next moment he was gone to wherever true heroes go.

Maggie and I hope to enjoy many more fishing seasons together, but tomorrow she could be plucked from our yard by a cougar, as with our little Aussie terrier, or I might keel over from some insidious bomb ticking inside. We can plan, but we never truly know. All we can do is welcome each new sunrise, be thankful for the gifts we've been given, and hope for more blessings as we travel life's winding path.

The final chapter of our love affair has yet to be written. I accept that our book is closer to the end than the beginning, but Maggie doesn't know it. She lives every day as if it's her only day. It's a lesson for all of us. We often sit together beside the stream these days, shoulder pressed to shoulder, watching the trout finning in the current. We don't always need to catch them anymore; it's enough to know they are there and that we could catch them if we wanted. I have come to realize that for many, perhaps most, fishing isn't about the fishing at all. Rather, it is about salving the sores rubbed raw by the friction of life. And with the right partner, fishing is about sharing, bonding, and most importantly, about love.

*Lou Phillippe lives on a trout stream in the Colorado mountains with his wife and three dogs. He has been fly fishing for a half century, and in between casts he is a contributor to a number of*

national and international outdoor magazines, which helps finance his fishing and hunting problem. His late father served in World War II in the Army Air Corps, and taught him to fish, read, and appreciate a good dog at the age of four. He has been the partner of several special dogs, but none so wonderful as the one-eyed yellow fishing dog, Maggie.

# Healing Waters and PTSD

## Tony Seahorn

How do we mend a wounded body or soul? How do we take a step forward in healing a spirit that has been battered by the trauma of battle? One possibility is to introduce the wounded warrior to a place of cooling waters, a place where fish are abundant and one can float through the waters that hum a soothing lullaby of serenity. Project Healing Waters is a volunteer organization that is dedicated to supporting the mending process of military personnel and vets who have been impacted by the effects of combat, and it uses wilderness waters and fishing to achieve its mission.

The idea originated when its founder, Ed Nicholson, an older vet, was being treated at Walter Reed Medical Center in Washington, D.C., when he noticed the numerous young people sitting idly in the waiting room. So, Ed decided to invite several to go fishing with him. On that first excursion, he discovered how this simple fishing experience made a huge difference both physically and emotionally with the young vets. Where eyes were once vacant, there was now a light of excitement; where

physical energy was almost stagnant, a resurgence of vigor returned; and where a life seemed consumed by pain and hopelessness, Mother Nature breathed her message of rebirth and Trust into the mind, heart, body, and soul of the wounded warrior.

Ironically, the Healing Waters Foundation has found that their greatest challenge is getting Wounded Warriors to the program. Recruitment is a huge obstacle, partly because of the physical and emotional needs of the individuals, and partly because of the legal ramifications of the vet centers/hospitals treating the individuals. Gosh, I had never imagined the number of logistical barriers organizations that wish to support our vets face.

Project Healing Waters tries to work through a VA therapist to identify prospective clients. By having a solid system in place, both the support organization and the VA centers can offer a clearer, more holistic approach to healing. The intervention received by the vet can then be measured and assessed as to what works best and why. This knowledge can then be shared with other VA centers and hospitals across the United States.

Ancient cultures have long understood that wounds of the body and soul need a holistic approach for healing to occur. Medications, cognitive therapies, surgeries simply aren't enough. Where medications have some difficult side effects, nature offers only blessings. Where daily life often brings disorder, there is order in nature—a way in which all things seem divinely connected from a single rain drop to a flowering mountain meadow. Where days feel misaligned, nature realigns the soul and spirit letting us know that all is as it should and can be. And, where our day by day activities may seem bounded by the constraints of too many to-do lists and responsibilities, nature chants a song of freedom, encouraging us to spread our wings and soar, even if these wings feel shattered.

So, if you are a disabled vet, knock down the door of your local VA center or hospital and beg, demand, barter with your medical personnel to get you aligned with a volunteer from Healing Waters.

Healing Waters volunteers serve as guides, coaches, and companions to our

country's wounded warriors. Their mission is uncomplicated—it is merely about healing and mending minds, bodies, and spirits one unhurried cast at a time on one soothing river somewhere in America. Casting, Healing. Casting, Healing. Casting, Healing, and the wounds begin to slowly mend.

*Following his tour of duty in Vietnam and subsequent physical therapy and recovery from combat wounds, Tony was informed by the Army that permanent nerve damage to his arm and shoulder would not allow him to pursue his dreams as a career aviator. After discharge from the service, Tony made a career in management with AT&T where he was able to finish his college education and went on to get an MBA. Recently retired, he and his wife Janet started their own education consulting and outdoor adventure business, Team Pursuits. Following encouragement from family and friends, his most honored medals from combat are now displayed in a shadow box in their home, including two Bronze Stars for heroism, two Purple Hearts, an Air Medal for Valor in Flight, a Vietnamese Gallantry Cross, and a Presidential Unit Citation. When not traveling and writing, Tony spends much of his time training two overly enthusiastic black Labs, Chase & Hunter Bailey. They love to bird hunt, fly fish, and help guide the raft downriver.*

*Tony and Janet co-authored the book Tears of a Warrior, which is being used by VA Hospitals and Vet Centers around the country to help veterans and families heal from the wounds of war. Visit www.tearsofawarrior.com.*

# Acknowledgments

As I wade the streams and lakes in northern Colorado and southern Wyoming, I am forever grateful to those who touched my life and encouraged me to get outdoors and experience the joy of fly fishing. It is a joy that expands with each trip taken, fish caught or not, and with every friend I meet along the way.

Special thanks to my father, Cecil Miller, whose passion and knowledge of fishing he shared with my brothers and me. To my mother, Jeannine Van Scoy, who with great patience read my early fishing essays and provided "tough love" editing in those beginning days. Also, to my wife Laura, who has given up countless hours of our time together so I could serve our nation's heroes.

To Jennifer Top, owner of TulipTree Publishing, for believing in and supporting this project from conception to completion. Your guidance has been invaluable.

Much of what is written in this book wouldn't happen without the selfless work from thousands of volunteers who make Project Healing Waters Fly Fishing the successful program that it is. I've made too many friends to list in the last five years that I've worked in the program. One who deserves recognition, and my thanks, is Duane Cook, Project Lead for the Platte Rivers Chapter of PHWFF. We first met three years ago to discuss starting this chapter, which has grown to be the largest program in the United States. In 2015, our chapter members and volunteers logged over 16,000 road miles taking veterans and active duty military personnel fly fishing, taught fly tying classes, performed fund-raising, and more. It is an honor for me to call Duane a friend.

Thanks to all the authors and writers who contributed to this anthology. Something special happens when we go fly fishing, and then we put those moments into words to create a place where others can go and enjoy it, too. Nicely done, everyone.

Finally, thanks to Mother Nature and your beautiful creatures who welcome the wandering souls that venture in your world so that we may discover who we truly are. I pray we take good enough care of you so that future generations are as blessed as we are.